TIGER CAT

By C.K. Thompson, R.A.O.U., J.P.
(Member of the Royal Australasian Ornithologists' Union)

This edition published 2018
By Living Book Press

Copyright © The Estate of C.K. Thompson, 1952

Cover image by Ways.

The publisher would like to give a huge 'Thank You' to the author's family
for their assistance in making this book available once more.

ISBN: 978-0-6481048-7-2

A catalogue record for this
book is available from the
NATIONAL LIBRARY OF AUSTRALIA National Library of Australia

CONTENTS

DEDICATION

To my good friend FLORENCE EGAN, of Birmingham Gardens, N.S.W., in happy appreciation of family gatherings around the piano, and with special reference to Tschaikovsky's *Concerto No. 1 in B Flat Minor, Op. 23*, and Arlen's *El Alamein Concerto*. Yes, and even *12th Street Rag* and *Dark Town Strutters' Ball!*

AUTHOR'S NOTE

WANDERERS in the great Australian bushland are always enchanted by its many beauties, of which our native birds and animals enjoy a major share.

The bush, however, is a region of sheer contrast. What could be more diametrically opposed than the dainty fairy wren with his beautiful plumage, his engaging ways and jauntily cocked-up tail, and the lumbering, ugly-looking goanna? Aren't they first class, real-life examples of Beauty and the Beast?

But to the scientist, the zoologist, the ornithologist and the naturalist, there is charm in every living creature, even the crocodile and the snake. It must be remembered, too, that every animal and bird has its own place in creation and if we Australians are to gain a true appreciation of our unique fauna, we must learn all we can about all of them.

I doubt if many of my young readers will agree with me that there is anything interesting about snakes. Most people hate and fear them and kill them on sight. The golden rule, of course, is to leave snakes severely alone. The great majority of them are not aggressive unless provoked and are as anxious to get out of man's way as he is to get out of theirs.

There are about 160 different kinds of snakes in Australia, and of these about 100 are venomous. Reptile experts agree that the most dangerous are the Tiger Snake, the Death Adder, the Common Brown Snake, the Giant Brown Snake (Taipan) and the Copperhead, with the Red-bellied Black Snake the least deadly. Fortunately, the Taipan is restricted to parts of the far north.

Of the reptiles that are very plentiful all over Australia, scientists have established that the Common Brown Snake is the most dangerous and ferocious. One of Australia's foremost naturalists, Mr. Charles Barrett, F.R.Z.S., has referred to it as a "reptilian racehorse" which, for a short distance, if in top form in hot weather, can travel practically as fast as the average man is able to run.

From the rather unattractive subject of snakes we pass on to that much-abused little marsupial, the Bandicoot, which you will meet in Chapter Four.

It is common for a person who does not like the ways of some other person to refer to him as being "as miserable as a Bandicoot." Far from being miserable, the Bandicoot is a friendly little fellow and very inoffensive to man; though among themselves Bandicoots can and do stage quite fierce fights.

While I was writing this book, I was told by a lady that one night she heard a noise in her garden and, flashing a torch, saw a Bandicoot busily digging up the lawn. It quickly fled. Next morning she found a small, hairless baby Bandicoot which apparently had been jolted from its mother's pouch when she took fright and bolted. This lady was one of the few people I have met who have a good word for the Bandicoot.

I passed on the incident to Mr. Ellis Troughton, F.R.Z.S., Curator of Mammals at the Australian Museum, Sydney, and Mr. Troughton wrote back to me that it was very hard at times to convince people that Bandicoots did little harm to gardens. He emphasised that the funnel-like pits are obviously dug for the Bandicoot to reach grubs and worms; also, that the jaws and teeth of the long-nosed local Bandicoot are so slender and the teeth so fragile, being intended by nature for a soft-bodied insect diet, that the little animal could eat only the softest of vegetable matter and then only occasionally, such as when food was put out for other animals.

So it will be seen that Bandicoots do not breakfast off beans, lunch off lettuces, dine off dahlias, or sup off spuds. Neither do they gnaw carrots.

It should be remembered that as the bushland in suburban areas gets smaller due to the spread of human habitation, the Bandicoot is forced to get his food where he can; so he invades gardens and lawns, sometimes in sheer desperation.

The incident in the last chapter in which Dasyure saw a Native Water-Rat dragging a Musk-Duck ashore in a creek, is authentic. Mr. Troughton records an observer as having seen a Water-Rat towing a full-grown Coot it had killed in the waters of Macquarie Swamps, N.S.W. The Coot, or Swamp-hen, is a very handsome bird with blue and black feathers, red bill and legs.

In Chapter Seven I have described how young Ted Holland had the wits scared out of him by the cry of a large Owl. Known variously as the Powerful Owl, the Winking or Barking Owl, its cry often has terrorised people in the bush at night.

Famous Australian ornithologist, Mr. A. H. Chisholm, F.R.Z.S., has described the cry as the most appalling sound uttered by any bird in Australia—something like the laughter of a demented Kookaburra.

I am confident, however, that all my young readers will agree with me that the good and the bad, the beautiful and the terrible, are fascinating combinations that make our great bushlands the very wonderful places they are.

You must, too, have a kindly feeling towards Dasyure as a fellow-Australian. Tiger Cats, Native Cats and the rest of the *Dasyuridae* family do a great deal of useful work in keeping down vermin from mice to rabbits.

Like a good Australian, Dasyure is fearless and courageous, ready to fight for what he thinks is right. And, like every good Australian, he is entitled to a "fair go"—as is every one of the very wonderful and useful native animals and birds in this great land of ours.

C.K. Thompson

CHAPTER ONE.
THE BUSH BURGLAR.

DASYURE, the tiger cat, was a handsome fellow and his brown body and tail, spotted over in white, was always sleek and clean. He lived in a hollow log which was wedged between two rocks in a thick tea-tree scrub, and terrorised the bush within a wide radius of his home. There was only one entrance to the log. The other end was jammed up against a big rock.

There was not one bird or beast that could scare Dasyure. A pugnacious animal, he would fight anything, whether he had to or not. He was both brave and bold and was not above taking on a creature he had no chance of beating.

Of course Dasyure, like his smaller relatives, the native cats, was not a cat at all. He did not even resemble a domestic cat very much. He ate flesh and he roamed at night, but he did not sit on rooftops or fences singing his love songs to the moon or to female tiger cats, or spend his nights squalling and howling and being made the target for old boots hurled by sleepless human householders. Above all, he was a marsupial, and was proud of the fact.

No, Dasyure had other things to do, and as he poked his nose from the hollow log and threw a wary eye around as much of his domain as he could see, he pondered thoughtfully upon where his first meal was coming from.

Dasyure was not very hard to please as to food. He liked young nestlings and he liked their parents, too. He had a taste for bandicoots, mice, birds' eggs and small lizards. He would even eat a frog if times were tough. A rabbit, big as it was, would meet with his hearty approval, and he was not the least bit averse to visiting a poultry run and sampling a fowl or two. He liked fish, but this was very hard to get.

He was not one of those animals who pushed themselves forward and sought publicity. Like a human burglar, whom he resembled a little in his habits, he was shy and retiring. There, however, the similarity ended. Burglars were not brave persons, but Dasyure was a brave animal—absolutely fearless.

Creeping out of the log, he paused and thoughtfully rubbed his whiskers with one of his front paws. It was dusk and time to begin the hunting round. Already the eager early stars were twinkling in the sky.

For most of the bush creatures, the time for rest and sleep had arrived, but for many others the serious business of living had just commenced.

Dusk in the bush was something like the changing of a shift at a big industrial works, where some men went home to rest while others began to work.

But there was no co-operation of that kind in the bush.

The worker in industry took up the tools another worker had laid down and there was a continuation of effort. The workers were friends and fellow employees, toiling for their own and for their country's prosperity. Among Dasyure and his kind, it was each for himself, and the tooth, the claw, the talon and the fierce beak for his neighbour. Kill or be killed.

Not one of the smaller birds or animals which settled

down to sleep each night in the bush had any guarantee that it would see another sun rise. During the daylight hours small birds and animals, in between collecting food for their young ones and themselves, had to keep a watchful eye on their homes and themselves lest hunting hawks, butcher birds, snakes, goannas and other marauders should turn them into a convenient meal.

That was bad enough, yet night's black wings were scant protection for them, because darkness brought with it the menace of prowling owls, nightjars, tiger cats, native cats and other devilish slayers. Truly, it was each for himself, only the fittest, and the luckiest, surviving.

Thoughts like these, of course, never entered Dasyure's head. He was out for what he could get all the time, and it was just bad luck for anything eatable that crossed his path.

He had little hope of finding a meal near his hollow log. No birds nested or roosted there. Dasyure saw to that.

There had been an occasion, long since, when a pair of blue wrens were indiscreet enough to build a nest in one of the tea-trees right near the hollow log. They were pretty little creatures—Bluecap in his resplendent plumage and his demure little brown mate. As they chirped and twittered about their nest-building, proudly and jauntily carrying their cocked-up tails, they presented a charming picture.

To Dasyure, lurking in his hollow log, their beauty made no appeal. To him they were merely a couple of mouthfuls of meat and as soon as the time was ripe, he intended to deal with them rather severely. The two wrens roosted near their nest at night, but Dasyure did not interfere with them. Neither were they troubled by any other prowling tiger or native cat. Dasyure was lord of all he surveyed in that area.

In due course the wrens laid their eggs and hatched three young ones. Dasyure waited until they were a fair

size and then one night he quietly climbed the tree and, in
two meals, ate them all. He got Bluecap asleep on a twig
near the nest and quietly ate him without disturbing the
rest of the family. The mother bird was surprised on the
nest and quickly disposed of. Then, licking his lips with
satisfaction, Dasyure leisurely returned to the ground and
went off hunting through the bush. On his return home
at dawn he scaled the tree and made an early breakfast of
the three nestlings.

Since then, no other birds had nested in the tea-trees which
sheltered the hollow log, or even within a wide radius of it.
Whether the news of the massacre had travelled through the
bush in some mysterious fashion and warned all the other
birds to give the place a wide berth, is not known.

Dasyure had been born in that hollow log and had lived
there all his life. He had taken it over from his mother after
she had been killed. When that tragedy had occurred, he
himself was only half-grown.

She had been a fine old mother, and had reared successive
litters of kittens during her long life; but not in this hollow
log. She had been something of a wanderer, sometimes
making her home in a hole among rocks, sometimes in a
small cave, sometimes in a hollow tree trunk. She had even
used a deserted wombat's hole at one period.

The log in which Dasyure was born was destined to be
her last home. The old tiger cat was feeling very tired of life,
but that did not cause her to take her maternal duties less
seriously. She kept watch and ward over her two kittens,
Dasyure and his sister. Though some tiger cats and native
cats were known to have as many as seven kittens in a litter,
the most she had ever had was five and the least, two—
Dasyure and his sister.

Both of them were very attractive little animals and when

they were old enough to leave their mother's pouch and run about, often played with each other like domestic kittens.

Their hard bush training commenced as soon as they were old enough to learn. The natural caution which was inborn in every bush animal was most marked in the tiger cats. During daylight hours they mostly slept and therefore were of little trouble to their mother. At night, however, it was a different proposition. The kittens, though young, were as equally creatures of the night as she was, and therefore apt to wander. But they didn't. They stayed in that log ready to receive any tasty tid-bits their hunting mother might bring to them.

And rarely did she fail. If the hunting was good, then they benefited considerably; if a meal had been hard to find, they had to go on short rations; but the old tiger cat put her children first. She did not eat until their hunger had been satisfied or, if not satisfied, at least allayed. She went hungry herself before they did. The tiger cat family in the old hollow log was reduced to two in distressing circumstances.

One night while out hunting, the old mother came across rabbit sign and felt quite excited. Though rabbits abounded all over Australia, this particular piece of country was singularly free of them.

The old cat did not know the reason for this and did not care, but the rabbits around here had been practically exterminated by every method a determined settler could employ.

The bushlands were extensive and, in parts, very dense, but a few human settlers had carved homes out of the scrub and had cultivated the land. These farms were miles apart, the nearest—to the hollow log—being about two miles away. This was owned by a farmer named Jack Holland, who lived there with his wife and sturdy young son Ted, and worked the property with the aid of a farm-hand and also with the minimum assistance of young Ted. The boy worked only when he could not dodge it.

Mr. Holland, when he first started to clear the land, noticed a few rabbit burrows and determined to wage war on the pests from the very outset.

"They don't appear to be very numerous here, and I don't intend that they should be," he told his farm-hand, Dave Chisholm. "We'll dig them out and we'll poison them. I've had experience of these things in other parts. Once they get the upper hand, you may as well chuck the game in. In the outback they have practically eaten the heart out of the country. Well, they're not going to do it here. This land cost me a lot of money and I'm going to get it back with crops. Those crops are going to feed us and to feed the people. I'm not going to raise produce and grain simply in order that useless rabbits may live well."

So Holland and Chisholm waged war on the rabbits, setting traps, using poison, digging them out, blasting them skywards and generally making their lives miserable—if they had any lives left to make miserable. The result was that not one rabbit was left in the area by the time Holland's first crops were ready for harvesting. As to the future, however, he had his doubts, and frankly admitted them.

"They'll come again, Dave," he told Chisholm. "You can't keep rabbits down for good. If everyone acted as we have done, there would be a good chance, but most farmers let them rip and hope for the best."

That had been two years previously when the old tiger cat had not been a resident of the district. At that period she lived in another hollow log many miles to the west. It was good country from her point of view and she probably would have been content to stay there if conditions had remained unaltered. But they did not.

During the hot summer a bushfire destroyed her hollow log and nearly destroyed her too. Fortunately, the pungent smoke which drifted into her sleeping quarters drove her into the open and away through the burning bush until she found a safe refuge among some rocks. After that adventure, she decided to leave the district for good, and eventually arrived in her new domain and established her home in the present hollow log.

Rabbits, of course, were not new to her. She had killed and eaten many before and had found them greatly to her taste. That was the reason she felt so pleasantly excited when she happened upon the trail of one on this particular night.

The bunny that had made the trail was nowhere in sight, but that was a minor detail. Cautiously the old tiger cat followed the trail which led across a grass patch and through some bushes. When the old hunter slid into these and pushed her nose through, she was rewarded with the sight of the prey nibbling the grass not three feet from where she crouched.

All unconscious of impending disaster, the rabbit continued to feed. The tiger cat silently slid from the bushes and flattened herself to earth. The night was pitch dark and a light breeze which stirred the leaves of the trees and sighed softly through the bushes and undergrowth, aided the hunter in her design. The rabbit certainly had ears long enough to catch any sound, but those ears played it false tonight. It did not hear the cat and, as it had its back towards her, did not see her.

When the marauder was within two feet of the unsuspecting bunny she made one leap and landed on its back, immediately sinking her sharp teeth into its neck. The rabbit gave one sharp squeal and died, its assailant's teeth still buried in its soft flesh.

The rabbit was not fully grown, which made it easier for the tiger cat to transport. Half-carrying and half-dragging it, she set off for home, eventually reaching the log, where two pairs of shining eyes greeted her as she entered.

The three tiger cats, old and young, dined sumptuously that night. There was more than enough for all and Dasyure, a bit of a glutton, ate so much that he fell asleep with a mouthful still unswallowed. The old mother did not stint herself either, but the other youngster, who was feeling a little off colour, ate sparingly.

There was no more hunting that night. It was unnecessary.

When daylight came, the three cats were sound asleep, but Dasyure's sister was a little restless. She was still not feeling very well. Her mother and brother, who had both eaten so heartily of the rabbit, were sleeping off the effects of that meal, but she had no effects to sleep off.

Presently she awoke, yawned and stretched herself. A glance showed her that the rest of the family were still in a very deep sleep. She prodded Dasyure with her paws in a half-hearted attempt to wake him up and invite him to play with her, but he was unresponsive. Then she began to tweak her mother's tail. The old cat took no notice, nor did she awaken when the younger female climbed over her and began to creep down the log towards the entrance.

Had the old mother not been so fast asleep she would have awakened instinctively and checked her offspring. Both Dasyure and his sister had been warned time and time again that they must not leave the hollow log alone, especially during the daytime. Dangers abounded on every side, especially when the sun was up. In any case, it was not the right time for tiger cats to be abroad. Work at night, sleep during the day. That was the routine and had been ever since the first tiger cat had appeared in the bush.

The young cat reached the entrance to the log and blinked at the strong sunlight outside. For a moment she hesitated, changed her mind, and returned to where Dasyure was sleeping. Again she tried to awaken him, this time to invite him to share in her adventure, but he did not stir. She looked at her mother thoughtfully, but did not attempt to awaken her. She knew what the old lady's views would be on such a crazy suggestion that they should go wandering around in the sunlit bush.

The only excuse that can be offered for the young cat is that she was not feeling very well and therefore did not quite know what she was doing. Had she had her wits completely about her, she might not have ventured into the open. On the other hand, being a female, she possessed the waywardness of her sex and, therefore, was unpredictable.

Be that as it may, she did leave the hollow log, and did creep out into the sunlight. What is more, the young villain actually enjoyed it. As the warmth penetrated her fur, she began to feel better. This, she told herself, was a bit of all right. What harm was there in it? Why had her mother been so insistent that neither she nor Dasyure venture into the daylight? Why, it was very pleasant out here. It was always the same with grown-ups: they hated to see their children having a good time.

All around her the bush was quiet, and danger seemed to be very far away. The only living thing she could see was a small skink lizard, which scampered across the hard ground in front of her.

Presently she decided to go for a stroll and to do a bit of exploring. It could only be described as a stroll, because she did not adopt any of the most elementary precautions. She just marched along carelessly, as if the whole bush belonged to her.

And that was her undoing.

About half a mile from the hollow log she came upon a heap of rocks and scrambled up on top of them. The warm sun continued to beat down upon her and was so pleasant that she stretched herself on top of a flat rock and blinked herself into a lazy doze. Her illness, or whatever it was that had upset her, had disappeared and although she knew full well that she should be back in the hollow log with the rest of the family, she was too comfortable to move.

Now, just above her head and a little to the left, was a ledge of rock covered with tufts of grass. Presently two of these tufts began to waver and tremble as if stirred by a gentle breeze—but there was no breeze blowing. Then, between the two tufts, a flat head slowly projected itself and two wicked eyes glared down upon the unsuspicious young tiger cat not two feet away. The head belonged to a carpet snake—twelve feet of it—and in the small animal below, the reptile, which had been fasting for quite a long time, saw a convenient meal.

Raising its head and retracting it so that the first few feet of its body could form a spring, the snake suddenly struck forward and downward, its head hitting the unfortunate tiger cat and crushing the life out of it. The reptile then picked up the body in its capacious mouth, withdrew to its own ledge of rock and there settled down to enjoy its easily-won feed. It would take some time to swallow and digest the young animal, but the carpet snake was in no hurry and had no other plans or engagements for the day.

CHAPTER TWO.
DASYURE GOES HUNTING.

THE DISAPPEARANCE of her young daughter was accepted by the old mother tiger cat as just one of those things that occur in life. In any case, the time had been fast approaching when both youngsters would have had to get out and fend for themselves. She was getting too old now to be bothered with them. Still, the youngster had been rather young, really, to leave home. However, there it was, and nothing could be done about it.

Such was the attitude of the old mother, but Dasyure missed his sister a little. They had had great games together in the hollow log. He wondered vaguely what had become of her, but as the days slipped by she became a dim memory and then not even that.

Dasyure was now old enough to go out at night with his mother to learn hunting lore, and the old cat taught him a lot. He was quick to learn, but the pair often went hungry. At times Dasyure was too eager and too impatient and often missed his prey, while his mother, being well past her prime and far from agile now, could hunt down only the easiest of meals. Birds' eggs, when she could find any, small lizards trapped unawares, and even frogs, were converted into food. Dasyure did not take kindly to frogs, but they were better than nothing. Anyway, he was a better hand at catching them than his mother was. There was one good thing about frogs—one did not have to climb tall trees to get them. That was hard work, especially for the old mother.

Conditions—and meals—improved as Dasyure improved, which he did, rapidly. Natural instinct and habit came to his aid, supplying what his mother either could not or would not.

Of course, Dasyure should have been thrown out of the hollow log a long time ago to find his own home and go his own way, but the elder tiger cat couldn't be bothered with that. The log was big enough for them both and she had no intention of seeking another mate. Another and very strong point was that she had to rely upon her fast-growing son for sustenance.

On his side, the young tiger cat was content with the arrangement, but there were occasions when he felt that he should not have to do most of the hunting.

They were out one night in the bush not a great distance from home when they came to a gum tree in which Dasyure felt convinced there was something to eat. What it was, he did not know, but something deep down inside him kept insisting that he scale the tree and explore it. He did so. His mother stayed on the ground and watched his progress with interest and anticipation.

Presently he was lost to sight among the leaves and branches, so the old cat crept across to the trunk of another tree about twenty yards away, with some vague idea of scaling it to see if there was anything worthwhile up it. She climbed a couple of feet and then decided to give it best. Dropping back to earth again, she sat on her haunches and began to lick her whiskers.

In the meantime, Dasyure had reached the first branch and was about to climb up higher when he noticed a dark blob squatting on it about six feet from the trunk. He could not make out what it was. Whether the small animal saw him or not, it suddenly gave expression to a gurgling shriek which ended in a stream of bubbling sounds, which momentarily startled the tiger cat.

The noise-maker was a glider-possum, one of the most graceful little marsupials in the bush. It was sitting there having a light meal of leaves and attending entirely to its own business.

Distinguished from its common ring-tailed relation by its ability to spread its body parachute-fashion and volplane like a child's toy aeroplane, the glider-possum had nothing much to fear from the tiger cat, provided it saw the cat first and had a clear field of escape. Whereas the ring-tail had a long and tapered tail, the prehensile end of which was usually curled in a ring owing to its constant use in gripping branches when climbing, the glider's tail was fluffy and he used it as a rudder when he was flying.

Dasyure considered that the possum would repay closer inspection, so he began to creep along the branch towards it. The glider, however, saw him coming and, again uttering its rather unearthly shriek, stayed not upon the order of its going, but went.

Spreading out its graceful body and with its tail stuck straight out behind, it glided downwards swiftly, intending to land near the base of the nearest tree and then scale up it.

Unfortunately, the tree for which it was making was the one at the foot of which Dasyure's mother was sitting, and it was either stupidity or ignorance on its part that made the glider utter its cry again while it was in mid-air. This drew the old cat's attention to it. She saw it bearing down upon her and was ready for it.

With its body flattened out so that it looked something like a miniature mat, the possum glided swiftly downwards and then, in order to make a safe landing, straightened out and looped upwards, intending to land on the tree trunk a few feet from the ground. But as it did so, the old mother cat, summoning what was left of her strength, sprang wildly into the air, her claws outstretched, and literally tore the possum to earth where a quick bite deprived it of its life.

Dasyure, up on the branch, had watched the proceedings with interest. It was the first glider-possum he had seen and he took it to be some kind of bird.

His interest gave way to real pleasure when the old tiger cat captured the little marsupial, and as quickly as he could, he scrambled down the tree and rushed to her side to get his share of the prey.

Great was his amazement and deep was his indignation when his mother, the possum beneath her paws, flattened back her ears, bared her teeth in snarling rage and indicated as plainly as she could that he was not going to get any more than a look and, possibly, a free smell, of the meal.

Well, thought Dasyure, this was a nice state of affairs, this was! This was maternal gratitude for you! Who had been the main food collector in recent weeks? Not her! Hadn't he worked his paws down to the very claws hunting so that they both might eat? He certainly had, and, by the flowering gum trees, he was going to eat now!

Returning snarl for snarl and threat for threat, Dasyure advanced upon his mother in a menacing manner. The old cat did not budge one single inch. She intended to stick to that glider-possum and fight for it to the death if necessary. She might be old and tired, she might be past her prime, but she was still a tiger cat, and no tiger cat had ever turned tail, especially when a meal was involved in the argument. The young whipper-snapper! Who did he think he was? He could consider himself lucky she hadn't tossed him out of their hollow log long ago.

Dasyure crept right up to his mother and made a noise which indicated that he wanted a piece of possum and that right speedily. He thrust out his nose until it almost touched his mother's and she deliberately spat in his face. Dasyure returned the insult. The old cat had both paws on the possum, but, raising one with a swift motion, she scratched Dasyure down the side of one cheek. The youngster snarled and gave back a couple of inches.

His mother watched him warily, fully prepared to turn the matter into a free-for-all fight if Dasyure persisted in his unwelcome cadging. But that intelligent young animal, his cheek smarting and his feelings wounded by his mother's heartlessness, decided to go no further into the matter.

Being a tiger cat, though only a young one, his instinct told him that he had no chance of getting that possum away from his mother. Of course, he could fight her for it and, no doubt, could beat her, but she could have the thing. There were plenty more in the bush. Anyway, if this was going to be her attitude, she could look after herself in future and do her own hunting. He was through with her and was going home.

The old tiger cat watched him narrowly as he slunk away through the bushes, and when she was certain that he had gone for good, she picked up the possum and proceeded homewards.

She had gone only a few yards, however, when it occurred to her that probably Dasyure, too, was making for the family log. If so, there would be more arguments over the ownership of the glider, and she didn't want that. She wanted the possum, not a fight, so, crawling under a low bush, she proceeded to eat the little marsupial.

She had absolutely no maternal feeling or love for Dasyure. It had been different when he was a small, helpless kitten. Now he was merely another tiger cat and, what was more, a tiger cat that had tried to deprive her of a meal she had won entirely by her own efforts. She hadn't stolen it from him, had she? Who did he think he was, anyway?

Her hunger satisfied for the time being, the old cat went off through the scrub and presently came to a track that wound more or less in the direction of the hollow log. She slunk along this and in due course arrived at a small, open, sandy patch of ground.

She was crossing this without any thought of danger to herself when something stirred beneath her feet, something with a very broad head and a stout, yellowish-brown body about two feet long. The old tiger cat skipped high and sideways, but, quick as she was, the death adder was quicker. It struck like a lightning flash, its deadly fangs penetrating her face near her whiskers. Then it drew backwards and glided off into the thickets.

In a few seconds it was all over with the old hollow log dweller. The deadly poison worked quickly and her sightless eyes did not see the early light of the rosy dawn that heralded another day.

The hollow log now belonged to her son, who, still smarting under the indignity he had suffered, was hunting around the bush for something to eat.

Dasyure managed to obtain a meal in a rather unusual manner. He was creeping disconsolately in the direction of home when, at the foot of a banksia, he saw, moving very feebly on the ground, a small, blind, featherless bird. Where it had come from, he did not know, but where it was going to, he knew full well. He was licking his chops and wishing heartily that it had been six times the size it was, when something struck him lightly on the back. He gave a startled leap and then noticed another quivering little morsel. That, too, went the same way as the first, with no questions asked.

The first act of the drama that had provided this unexpected feed had been played in the banksia tree several weeks before when a pair of honeyeaters had built their nest and, in due time, had laid their eggs. Their nestbuilding had been closely observed and followed by a bronze cuckoo, which had bided its time. It intended in the fullness of time, to make those honeyeaters hatch and rear its own offspring, which was the pleasant habit of cuckoos.

When the time was ripe, the cuckoo laid its egg on the ground, picked it up gently in one claw and, flying to the honeyeaters' nest, placed it therein. Then it picked up one of the honeyeaters' eggs and flew off with it, dropping it carelessly a quarter of a mile away. The honeyeaters still had three eggs, but only two of them were their own.

The young cuckoo was the last to be hatched. The baby honeyeaters were each twenty-four hours old before he pecked and pushed his way out of the egg. And that was the beginning of the end for the rightful occupants of the nest.

He was not quite twenty-four hours old himself when he began to resent the presence of the two little unfledged honeyeaters. Though he, like them, was blind and only a quivering mass of flesh, he was much bigger and he wanted the nest to himself. So he wriggled and manoeuvred around until he succeeded in getting a nestling on to his back when, with a convulsive heave like a miniature bucking horse, he literally catapulted the little honeyeater out of its nest. That was the small morsel Dasyure had found under the tree.

And, though the tiger cat did not know it, while he was eating that morsel, the young cuckoo in the nest above him was preparing to eject the second honeyeater, and did so.

Dasyure went home to his hollow log and went to sleep, but he had it in mind to visit that banksia tree again. Any tree that rained young birds was worth keeping under observation.

He wondered vaguely what had become of his mother, but her absence did not worry him.

He was back at the banksia tree at dusk. It was his first port of call after leaving home. For a long time he sat at the foot of the tree waiting patiently for small birds to fall out of it again, but nothing like that happened.

At last he grew impatient and resolved that if a cheap meal were not going to come to him, he had better go and look for it. He decided to climb the banksia and see what it had to offer.

He saw the nest on a branch only a few feet from the ground and as he looked it over, two small birds flew away in terror, twittering loudly as they did so. Dasyure looked after them in mild surprise, tinged with disappointment and then, creeping along the limb, poked his nose into the nest. There lay the young cuckoo. Quickly the tiger cat seized the helpless young bird and, withdrawing along the limb, scrambled down the trunk to earth where he made short work of the youngster.

That done, he set off through the scrub to see what he could find in other parts.

CHAPTER THREE.
THE EGG COLLECTOR.

A REGULAR VISITOR to the Holland farm during the spring was Mrs. Holland's brother, Andrew Mitchell, who was a well-known naturalist. Though his sister always welcomed him with open arms, Mr. Holland regarded his visits with mixed feelings. He liked Andrew and they were the best of friends but, as he told his wife ruefully, young Ted was worse than useless when Uncle Andy was visiting. He never did much work around the place at any time, and when his uncle was there he did none at all.

The youngster, of course, hailed his uncle's arrival with great glee because it meant long rambles in the bush with him. Jobs to be done around the farm were forgotten and Ted's father, though he grumbled a lot, did not have the heart to interfere with the lad's happiness.

Uncle Andy announced that he was there on this occasion to study the habits of parrots and especially cockatoos.

There were scarcely any parrots living close to the farm, but occasionally a flight of blazing colour would sweep through the trees and reedy parrot calls echo around the bushlands. They never stayed long, these bright-plumaged birds. Perhaps it was because they did not like the food to be found there; perhaps it was a little too close to human habitation for them.

Young Ted's eyes shone whenever he saw them—blue and yellow rosellas, red-winged parrots, lories, parakeets, Corellas and many other representatives of the vast parrot tribe.

It must be confessed, however, that the lad's interest was taken up, not so much with the birds themselves—although he was a bird-lover—as with the eggs they laid. He was a great collector of birds' eggs and no number of threats on the part of his parents that they would "throw the rubbish into the fire" deterred him. Uncle Andy did not discourage the lad in his hobby, but he did impress upon him two rules... he must never destroy or harm a nest, and he must not take more than one egg from any nest. If he came across a nest with only one egg in it, he had either to leave it alone, or wait until the birds had added to their clutch.

And young Ted never broke those rules.

If the bush near the farm were devoid generally of parrot life, the white cockatoo with his distinctive sulphur-coloured crest was a permanent inhabitant, not of the farm or the nearby bush, but close enough to be a perfect nuisance to the farmer.

Away across the creek and the gullies were many tall trees and in these the white birds lived, or rather roosted. They spent a great deal of their time plundering crops. Much further out, over the plains, the galahs swarmed. They rarely came into the bushlands. Snowy, the white cockatoo, and his gang, instead of being thankful for this and returning good for good, were not above going out, in the grain season, and raiding the galahs' domain.

Old Snowy was no fool. He reasoned things out for himself. If he found a new scarecrow on the Holland property, he would advise his mates to keep away while he alone investigated. He would fly closer and closer to the supposed enemy, eyeing it carefully, until finally he would perch on it with a triumphant squawk which told the flock that all was well. In next to no time, a white mantle would settle on the crops.

But just because there was no danger from the scarecrow, it did not mean that Snowy was satisfied. He posted sentries all around the field, in trees and on fences, to give the alarm if danger threatened.

When Snowy and his gang of grain-bandits descended upon a crop, it was as if there had been a fall of snow.

And, when they had had enough, they arose in a white cloud that seemed to fill the sky. Uncle Andy found this of intense interest. So did young Ted. His father, however, had a different opinion.

"Why should I plant crops just to feed a lot of hungry cockatoos?" he asked in complaining tones. "It appears to me that I'm a sort of all-the-year-round Father Christmas in these parts. I rear poultry for foxes and tiger cats, grain for cockatoos and crops for rabbits and bandicoots."

"Bandicoots don't eat crops, Jack," said Uncle Andy. "They exist mainly upon insects and grubs."

"Well, I wish somebody would tell them that," grunted Mr. Holland. "It would save a few of my young seedlings and plants, no doubt."

"Ever seen a bandicoot eating your plants, Jack?" asked Uncle Andy.

"No, I have not. I've better things to do than sit up all night looking at bandicoots digging holes. I leave that to certain folk who go in for that kind of foolishness," snorted the farmer.

"Like me?" grinned Uncle Andy.

"Yeah, like you, Andy," assented Mr. Holland.

"But, listen, Jack, you've got it all wrong about bandicoots eating your plants," said Andy Mitchell earnestly. "They might uproot one or two seedlings but only while they are digging for their natural food of worms, grubs and beetles."

"I've seen plants bitten off," said Holland.

"Probably by cut-worms or snails, and bandicoots eat cut-worms, you know," said Mitchell. "They also are very fond of curl-grubs, which are the larvae of a beetle. These grubs eat the roots of grass. Bandicoots do good in orchards, too. They eat the fruit-root weevil which feeds on the roots of citrus trees. You've got to be tolerant, Jack, and not blame animals for what they do not do."

"I suppose you'll deny that the things are full of ticks, eh?" demanded the farmer.

"Oh, they carry ticks all right," admitted the naturalist, "but so do poultry and rats. If there were no bandicoots at all, there would still be ticks. There is this point, too — the more ticks in the bandicoots, the less there will be in your fowls.

"Anyway," went on the naturalist with a grin, "if you did the right thing and put up rabbit-proof fences around the farm, you'd keep the bandicoots out, as well as the rabbits."

"They'd only burrow under the wire," said Holland.

"No, they would not. Bandicoots don't go in for burrowing. But why don't you get a fox terrier? He'd keep the bandicoots in check."

"We've got a dog already, Uncle Andy," put in young Ted.

"That useless animal couldn't catch a cold," snorted his father.

Early next morning, Uncle Andy and young Ted set out on their cockatoo expedition. Uncle Andy, who had been everywhere in his study of bird life, told the youngster that on one occasion he took a trip on a Murray River steamer.

At night, when the bright headlights shone on the gum trees where the cockatoos roosted, it dazzled them, sending them screeching and protesting across the river to find another sleeping place in the friendly darkness.

Snowy and his mates had their nests in the tall gum trees by a swamp miles away from the Holland farm and it was there that Uncle Andy intended to seek them out and study their habits. They made their nests in holes in the trunks or hollow branches. They were wise enough, if pursued, to go into holes where there were no nests, baffling those hunters who thought they were on an easy thing. It was rather difficult to find Snowy's eggs or young family. Snowy saw to that.

Snowy had a cousin—Inky, the black cockatoo—but Inky was a complete stranger to his white relative. He favoured the coastal districts and adjacent ranges and was not a crop raider. He liked the seeds of trees and doted upon the wood-boring grubs that lived in the gums. Inky had a very powerful bill with which he ripped off bark and chopped into the wood to get at the grubs. No grub that ever bored a hole in a tree was safe from the black cockatoo. These birds did not get around in big flocks, preferring to pair off, though at times several would live together sociably.

Inky was as black as night. That was why young Ted had so named him; but he was not entirely black, his yellow tail relieving his sombre appearance. His plumage shone in the sunlight and his crest had gleams of yellow in it.

Rare indeed were Inky's visits to the farm, and so far away from it did he build his nest in the highest tree he could find, that Ted had never succeeded in finding one. He hoped his luck would change one day.

Ted tramped along cheerfully as he listened to his uncle talking about the cockatoos.

Passing down a bush track, they came to a small, open, sandy patch and were brought to a halt by what they saw lying on the ground.

"Gee, Uncle Andy, that looks like a dead cat, but it's a funny sort of colour," exclaimed the boy.

"H'm," mused Andy Mitchell, looking down at the pitiful heap that once had been Dasyure's mother. "It is a sort of a cat but not the kind you mean. That's a tiger cat. Wonder what killed it?"

He squatted on his haunches at the side of the small, spotted body and looked at it keenly. Then he examined the ground in the vicinity. Presently he gave a low whistle.

"What is it, Uncle Andy? What have you found out?" asked the lad.

"This is very interesting, Ted. From the marks on the ground here I'd say that Mrs. Tiger Cat had been bitten by a snake. What a strange thing!"

"A snake? What kind of a snake?" asked Ted, looking around him cautiously. He was not afraid of snakes, being a bush boy, but he respected them and their deadly habits.

His uncle was carefully examining marks on the ground.

"See there?" he asked, pointing. "It looks as if there was a bit of a scuffle. Notice the marks there where the snake crawled away?"

"I wonder where it is now?" asked Ted, having another wary glance around.

"Far enough away, you can bet. As to what sort of snake it was, I'd say it was a death adder. They are nocturnal in their habits—that is, they prefer to get around in the dark. So do tiger cats and native cats. Death adders also like to bury themselves in sand or dirt. It is more than likely that the tiger cat trod on the adder without knowing it, and got bitten to death for its pains. I can't be sure of that, of course, but, knowing something about these snakes, I think it could be so."

"Death adders are the worst snakes in the bush, aren't they?" asked Ted. "Gee, I'd like some snakes' eggs to add to my collection!"

"You stick to birds' eggs, young fellow-me-lad, and leave snakes alone," advised his uncle sternly. "As to the death adder being the worst snake in the bush, it's a toss up between him and the tiger snake. The brown snake is no angel, either."

"I don't like snakes," said Ted, with a little shudder of distaste. "They are such creepy, crawly things."

"Very few people do like them," his uncle commented. "Yet they have a certain beauty and are most interesting to study. Plenty of people have queer ideas about snakes. Some of the reptiles are not nearly as awful as they are painted."

"I wouldn't mind a snake's egg for my collection, anyway," repeated Ted, whose mind generally ran upon this subject.

"Only a few snakes lay eggs, notably the pythons," said Uncle Andy. "The only poisonous snake to lay them is the brown snake, and I'd advise you to keep away from her. In fact, leave all snakes alone."

Mitchell told the boy that Australia's worst snake was the taipan, or giant brown snake of the Northern Territory and north-eastern Queensland. It reached a length of ten feet and was among the most deadly in the world. Fortunately it was confined to the north and was not widespread like the death adder and tiger snake.

"There are plenty of black snakes around," said Ted.

"They can be dangerous all right," said his uncle, "but they never look for trouble. As a matter of fact, I've always found them to be rather amiable and friendly."

"They can keep their friendship," said Ted with a shudder. "But I'd like one of their eggs."

"They don't lay eggs," said Mr. Mitchell.

"It's funny about snakes swallowing their young ones to save them from danger, isn't it, Uncle Andy?" asked the boy.

"Don't you swallow that yarn, my boy," said the naturalist. "If they did, the young ones wouldn't come out alive again."

Young Ted looked disappointed. He had always believed that story.

"It's strange about this tiger cat, though," his uncle commented, examining the body again. "I am willing to swear that a death adder got it. This is just the kind of ground in which an adder would lurk. Probably the cat was coming home late and had been so well fed that it was not too cautious. Probably it trod on the snake. Adders don't generally go looking for trouble, but when they are disturbed they strike like a flash."

"Yes," said Ted, for want of something to say. He was not passionately interested in snakes.

"The golden rule is to leave snakes alone and they will leave you alone, so remember that, young Edward," said Uncle Andy.

"I won't go playing with any snakes," Ted assured him, and added, "but what are we going to do with this dead pussy cat, Uncle? Just leave it here?"

"No, we'll bury it. And don't call it a pussy cat. It isn't. It is a tiger cat, or native cat, and is as much like a domestic cat as soap is like sawdust," said Mr. Mitchell.

They had no difficulty in scraping a hole large enough to accommodate the dead animal and into this the body was placed and then covered over. Uncle Andy dusted the dirt from his hands and announced that he was ready to proceed on the journey to the cockatoos' territory.

"That is the first tiger cat I have ever seen," young Ted said as they walked along. "I'm often in the bush but I've never seen any live ones."

"They are not very numerous and, anyway, they come out at night while you are in bed. They are not as common as the smaller native cat. A friend of mine has a tame one as a pet. He caught it when it was a small kitten and reared it up like an ordinary domestic cat. Native cats are intelligent little chaps and very bold. Some of them will fight anything. Tiger cats are much the same."

"I suppose, Uncle Andy, that those that live wild in the bush eat a lot of birds and their eggs, too?"

"Thinking of your blessed collection again, eh?" smiled the naturalist. "As a matter of fact, native cats and tiger cats do eat birds and their eggs when they can get them, but I doubt if they do a great deal of harm that way. A bigger menace to birds is the domestic cat gone wild. A lot of cats take to the bush, you know. However, they do not destroy poultry like native and tiger cats do when they get the chance. They visit fowlyards and do a lot of damage at times. The number of fowls they kill shows that they must do it for sport. I mean to say, you know the size of a native cat. Well, how on earth could one of them eat a dozen fowls? Yet a friend of mine lost that many in one night. The native cat or tiger cat, or whatever it was, probably intended to kill only one hen and have a meal off it, but after he made the kill, he must have lost his head, or the killing instinct was too great, for he went ahead and slaughtered the blessed lot."

"I'll have to tell Dad about that so he can guard our fowls," said Ted.

"With you around the place, surely that should not be necessary?" smiled his uncle.

"But I'm not awake all night," replied young Ted seriously.

His uncle smiled again, but did not comment upon that.

As they continued their journey, Uncle Andy told his

young nephew something about cockatoos.

"A lot of people regard black cockatoos as weather prophets," he remarked. "There is an old saying among bushmen: 'Rain within a fortnight and a wet day for every bird you see.' So, Ted, if you ever see a flock of ten black cockatoos, there will be ten days' rain within a fortnight."

"Gee, Uncle Andy, is that a fact?" exclaimed the lad.

"So the bushmen say," his uncle replied. "They also say that white cockatoos, when they post their sentries, warn them that if they do not do their jobs properly, they will suffer for it."

"I've often seen white cockatoos feeding around the farm and I've seen their sentries on the fences and in the trees, but I don't know what you mean about the birds making the sentries suffer," Ted said.

"Some bushmen insist that if cockatoo sentries fail to warn a flock of danger and that flock is attacked, the angry birds turn on the sentries and kill them," said the naturalist.

"I suppose that is only justice," was the boy's thoughtful reply.

Uncle Andy and Ted spent a happy day in the bush watching the cockatoos at work and at play. Ted did not add to his collection of eggs because his uncle would not let him climb the high trees to look for nests. The boy, however, was determined that one day he would go out himself and see what he could discover.

They arrived back at the Holland farm just on dusk—at precisely the same moment that Dasyure, miles away in the bush, was attending to the cuckoo nestling.

CHAPTER FOUR.
DASYURE GOES VISITING.

A S THE DAYS turned into weeks and the weeks into months, Dasyure lived his life and conformed to tiger cat routine. In this, he did not have any association with any others of his kind, simply because he was the only one of his species in the district. He had, at times, encountered representatives of his smaller tribal relatives, the native cats, but he had no association with them, nor they with him.

But there was plenty of competition in the food hunting game apart from the bush cats. Marauding hawks, eagles, butcher birds, snakes, goannas, owls and others, all preyed on small bird and animal life, and as it was each for himself and never mind anybody else, the keenest and most efficient hunters got the available meals.

It was during the autumn months that Dasyure found the competition strongest. As almost all of the smaller birds had finished breeding and their young ones were old enough to take care of themselves, nests visited by the prowling tiger cat invariably were empty. He could still make a meal of small lizards, an occasional frog and now and then a rabbit, but it was hard going—practically a paw-to-mouth existence.

On one interesting occasion he had a taste of fish and

approved of it greatly.

He had been prowling along the bank of the creek prospecting the reeds to see if he could find and rifle a bird's nest, when he saw the fish, a small, freshwater perch, lying on the bank. It had been dropped by a blue crane, or white-fronted heron, which had had an argument with a pilfering kookaburra.

The crane had caught the fish and the kookaburra had sought to steal it from him in the fashion of kookaburras.

In the unpleasantness that followed, the crane dropped the fish and made off, the kookaburra in hot pursuit. Neither had returned for the lost fish, which remained on the ground for the rest of the day and into the night. By the time Dasyure came across it, it was dry and stiff and covered with ants. He smelled it, liked the aroma and ate it.

After that, he often prowled around that spot on the creek bank, but he never got another fish. And as he was never likely to obtain one by his own unaided efforts, he had to remain fish-hungry.

It was pure chance one night that took him hunting in the neighbourhood of the Holland homestead.

He had been making his usual rounds without finding anything, and that was the motive that impelled him to go further afield. He yearned to find something of interest, and something of interest to Dasyure meant, of course, food.

It was a beautiful night. The moon, just past its full, hung high in the heavens, bathing the whole of the bush in soft, silver light.

Dasyure, however, was not the least bit interested in scenic beauty. His idea of loveliness was a huge feed.

He slipped under a stout barbed wire fence and crossed a paddock which contained two horses and four cows. These large animals he treated with indifference. He did not know what they were and he cared less. The six domestic animals did not even see Dasyure. Very few creatures did see that marsupial when he did not wish to be seen.

Presently he found himself in the shadow of a shed. He looked it over and did not think much of it, but when he stole round the corner and came in full view of a dog sitting on its haunches outside a kennel, he paused and then backed round the corner again out of sight.

Dasyure had never seen a dog before. He was not afraid of the thing, of course, but it was located in a place he desired to pass. Whatever it was he would fight it if it disputed his right of way, but he could see no sense in rashly dashing into the fray.

Poking his head round the corner again he took stock of the dog. Its kennel was under a tree and it was chained up. Not knowing this or, indeed, the meaning of chains and such things, the tiger cat was a little startled when the dog got up off its haunches, yawned and went into its kennel, causing the chain to rattle musically as it did so.

The dog out of sight, Dasyure decided to get a move on. He stole away from the shed and quietly slid across the open space in front of the kennel. If the dog saw him, it made no sign.

It was then that the tiger cat became aware of an attractive but elusive smell. There were birds around somewhere, judging by that scent, but birds he had never encountered before.

With his whiskers twitching in anticipation, Dasyure followed his nose and this brought him up against another shed. Skirting this, he found himself confronted with a yard enclosed with wire netting, the shed standing in one corner of it.

Peering through the netting, he saw, squatting in a row

on perches, a number of very large birds. He had never seen
their like before and they looked a bit too large for him to
tackle. He would determine that later, however, when he
had a closer look at them.

But here he met with a check. He couldn't get through
the wire netting. He poked and pried around it without
finding an entrance. He tried to shove his head under
it and was almost strangled for his pains. Then, in a far
corner, diagonally opposite the shed, he found that the
wire, at ground level, was loose. Shoving his head under it,
he succeeded in scrambling partly into the yard, and then
found himself wedged. With a convulsive heave of his back,
he arched the netting sufficiently to permit him to crawl
right into the yard.

Sneaking across to the shed, he closely scrutinised the
sleeping fowls. Yes, they certainly were big enough. Well,
the bigger they were, the more food they would provide.

The lowest perch was two feet above the ground and on
it were four hens huddled together in the centre, leaving
each end of the perch bare. With an agile leap, Dasyure
gained one end of the perch and sat there for a moment
facing the fowls and examining them with an expert, yet
wary eye. Though they were big birds, they did not look
very dangerous to him.

Creeping along the perch, he got close enough to the
nearest fowl to reach out and touch it with a paw. The
fowl slept on.

Dasyure was so close that he did not have to spring. He
merely leaned forward and bit the fowl on the neck. The
unfortunate bird died in its sleep and tumbled from the
perch to the ground. It had barely hit the earth before the
tiger cat was on top of it.

For a moment he toyed with the idea of trying to drag

the bird out of the yard and back to the safety of the hollow log, but as the log was far distant and he was very hungry, he decided to have a meal there and then. With sharp teeth and claws he began to tear into the feathers, and when he reached the soft flesh he set to work. Never before had he tasted anything so delicious. He forgot everything but the business in hand and when he had eaten all he could conveniently hold, he licked his chops with the keenest satisfaction.

Squatting on the floor of the fowlhouse, he glared upwards at the sleeping occupants of the perches and then some imp of devilment possessed him. Crouching down to gain the maximum momentum he launched himself at the nearest bird, his paws striking it on the chest and knocking it backwards.

The hen awoke and proceeded to state its views on the proceedings. Its loud squawks awoke the other fowls and they began to squawk and cackle, too. A couple of roosters, not to be outdone, started to crow as if their very lives depended upon it and then the dog came out of its kennel and added its discordant barking to the tumult.

Dasyure was not scared by the uproar, but something told him that he would be safer in the bush and away from the din. Swiftly he made his way to the hole in the wire netting, slipped under it and stole off across the yard the way he had come.

This time the dog saw him. To the dog he was a cat and the dog did not like cats. He redoubled his barking efforts and then nearly strangled himself trying to get off his chain. Dasyure slowed down and had a good look at the dog. He could see that something was restricting the animal in its movements and he felt inclined to stay there and jeer at it.

By this time the tumult was so great, with fowls cackling

and squawking, roosters crowing and the dog barking and snarling that something had to happen. It did.

Out of the house came the farmer and in his hand he carried a rifle. He made straight for the fowlyard and looked through the wire netting. Seeing nothing out of the ordinary, he went to a small gate, opened it, and crossed the yard to the fowlhouse. When he saw the dead hen on the ground, he used rather bad language, some of which was directed at the still barking dog.

Leaving the yard, Holland walked quickly towards the kennel, at the same time yelling out to the dog to shut up. The dog, its attention centred on Dasyure, ignored his master. The tiger cat was now squatting on its haunches and looking at the dog as if it found that animal's antics entertaining.

Holland came to an abrupt halt when he saw Dasyure. Though the light was good, he could not quite make out what it was. It looked something like old Tom, the family cat, and yet...

"Puss, puss, puss," he called in seductive tones. If it were old Tom, he didn't want to make the mistake of dropping it with a bullet. But if it were a fox or a native cat...

Dasyure looked up and saw the man. What in the name of fortune was this creature? It was Dasyure's first glimpse of a human being.

Uncertainly he stood up and Holland gave a curse.

"A confounded fox!" he exclaimed. "I might have known it! Well, I'll soon fix his clock for him!"

Raising his rifle he took a steady aim. There was only a distance of thirty feet separating him and Dasyure and it would need only one bullet to end the fowl killer's career, he told himself grimly.

There was a loud, air-shattering report and the earth

in front of the tiger cat suddenly erupted, throwing dirt into his face.

This was no place for him! He stood not upon the order of his departure, but fled, and before Holland had time to again press the trigger of the repeating rifle, the tiger cat was nowhere to be seen. He was heading at full speed for the bush and for the safety of his hollow log.

CHAPTER FIVE.

DEATH IN THE TREETOPS.

Isoodon, the bandicoot, dwelt among the high reeds on the bank of the creek in a nest he had contrived out of sticks, grass and leaves. He was a sturdy little chap with rounded ears and a long snout. The only burrowing he did was when he was hunting for food and he spent most of his waking hours at that.

Isoodon was a marsupial that liked to be left alone. His main desire in life was to have plenty to eat and he ensured this by digging holes in the ground. Many farmers and gardeners would have been only too willing to give him a permanent hole in the ground.

He was a much abused and much maligned little animal. Agriculturists who discovered funnel-shaped pits among their crops muttered to themselves just what they would like to do to the bandicoot responsible, while householders, finding similar holes in their lawns, wrote indignant letters to the newspapers about wretched and useless animals that ate their precious grass.

Of course Isoodon and his tribe did little damage to plants. His main diet was worms, beetle larvae, grubs and other insect-life which lived at and destroyed the roots of plants. He scratched his cone-shaped hole to accommodate his long snout in his search for insects and the amount of vegetable food he ate would not have kept him alive for a day.

But humans persecuted Isoodon and did so without even trying to find evidence in his favour.

The bandicoot left his stick and grass nest at twilight and, selecting a likely-looking patch of earth in a small clearing where cast earth betrayed the presence of worms, he set to work to excavate a hole, using his front paws with their sharp claws.

His first attempt brought him nothing, so he hopped a few feet and sank another shaft. He had dug only about an inch when he struck it rich—the wriggling tail of an earthworm. Quickly he plunged his long nose into the hole, seized the worm's end and drew it wriggling from the ground. Fastidious to a degree, he sat on his haunches and quickly ran the fingers of both hands milking fashion down the worm's length to get rid of the clinging dirt. Then he ate it.

Isoodon's third excavation revealed a black beetle. He regarded it thoughtfully for a moment or two as if in doubt as to its food value. The disturbed beetle did not wait to be seized and hauled from the pit, but scrambled out under its own power and was making quick time for the shelter of some grass when Isoodon sprang on it, pinning it down with a front paw.

Releasing it, he regarded it with distrust as it started to crawl away. Then he started to paw at it with both hands, backing away as he did so. Retreating slowly, he rolled the beetle with him until it had a rather used-up, unattractive appearance. Still he was not satisfied. He rolled it again and succeeded in rolling the life completely out of it.

While he was trying to make up his mind whether he should eat the thing or not, he was joined by another bandicoot. This was Perameles, his rather larger and longer-nosed relation, an inquisitive type, who wanted to know what Isoodon was up to.

Isoodon gave him no satisfaction, in fact he ignored his presence. Perameles inspected the beetle, or what was left of it, and had he been content with only an inspection, all may have been well; but Perameles could not keep his long snout out of things that did not concern him.

Isoodon was by nature a friendly little soul, but he found much to resent in the inquisitiveness of this long-nosed intruder. The beetle belonged to him, and if he decided to eat it, he would. On the other hand, if he decided to reject it, he would do so, but that did not mean that Perameles could have it.

So, when the long-nosed bandicoot began to roll the beetle towards himself so that he could inspect it at closer quarters, Isoodon jumped on him, striking him with his hind claws and deftly removing some hair and skin in the process.

To say that Perameles was surprised is understating it. He was astounded. He looked at Isoodon as if contemplating assault and battery on him, and then decided to leave for other and more friendly territory. But he was not going to escape so easily. Isoodon's fighting blood had been aroused and as Perameles moved away, he sprang on him again and in a rapid scrambling movement, tore some more hair out of his hide, this time with his front claws.

That was more than enough for the long-nosed bandicoot. He turned on his smaller attacker and with a cry that was something between a grunt and a squawk, rushed him with open mouth and tried to bite him. Isoodon also opened his mouth and kept it open. He did not try to bite Perameles, but made another flying leap at him. Perameles met him willingly enough and the two little animals fell to work, using both front and hind claws when they could get the chance. Skin and hair began to fly, especially hair. They were plucking each other like a poultryman plucking a fowl. Though Isoodon was smaller than Perameles, he was more aggressive and this partially made up for his lack of weight.

Perameles was getting the worst of it and decided to break off the engagement. He turned tail and made for the bushes, Isoodon in hot pursuit. Once he made a flying leap at his retreating enemy, but, sadly misjudging both the distance and his own powers, nose-dived into the dirt with an agonised squeak.

When he had collected his wits again, Perameles was about to enter the comparative security of a bunch of reeds. Isoodon made a rush and then recoiled in terror at what he saw.

Perameles had just reached the reeds when a menacing spotted shape flew out of them and smashed him to the ground. It was Dasyure. That optimist had been along the creek bank looking for stray fish when he had been attracted to the scene by the scufflings of the two little bandicoots. He was hiding in the reeds watching them and deciding how best to attack them when Perameles had saved him the trouble by literally rushing to his doom.

Isoodon took one brief look at his stricken cousin, or as much of him as he could see beneath the paws of the tiger cat, and then he fled for his life and did not stop until he had wriggled his way to safety between some rocks not far away. He had too much sense to return immediately to his stick and grass home which would have afforded but scant protection from an animal like Dasyure if the tiger cat decided to chase him.

Dasyure, when he had quite done with the unfortunate Perameles, slunk off through the bushes away from the creek and when he reached a large gum tree, leisurely scaled it and, reaching a large branch, stretched himself along it and relaxed. He intended to stay there until hunger returned or daybreak arrived. If the former came first, he would renew his hunting. If the latter, he would go home.

Though Dasyure was feeling well fed and well content, his vigilance was not relaxed. Though he was just pondering peacefully, he knew what was going on around him in the bush. A distant croaking that ended in a sudden loud squawk told him that a frog had fallen a victim to a prowling snake; the faintest rustling of wings he heard meant that a boo book owl or a tawny frogmouth had passed the tree in quest of prey; the slight movement in the tree somewhere above him meant...

Suddenly Dasyure was more than alert—he was quivering with anticipation. What did that slight movement above him mean? There was a nest up there, and that might mean nestlings!

In a few seconds he was climbing the tree trunk and three branches higher than the one on which he had been resting provided the support for what he was seeking—a platform of sticks and twigs lined with grass. It was the carelessly built, or carelessly thrown-together nest of a tawny frogmouth, and, squatting in the nest was an unguarded youngster.

It was a comical-looking young 'un, as frogmouth nestlings are. Covered with long white down which caused it to look like a toy bird made of cotton wool, it had a beak several sizes too large for it. Both its parents were away on hunting business, which was bad luck for it.

The young bird heard a slight noise and turned its large, innocent, golden eyes on Dasyure. That animal, crouched on the branch, returned the stare with golden eyes which were smaller and far from innocent.

Dasyure was telling himself that this was a gift from the gods. He crept along the branch and was almost within paw-reach of the nestling when something struck him on the head. He glared round savagely, and caught a glimpse of brown and grey wings. Father frogmouth had returned home.

Dasyure, intent on the nestling, had not heard a sound of the parent bird's arrival, but now it was here he was prepared to deal with it. Flattening himself on the branch and digging his hind claws into the bark, he waited for the next attack. It was not long in coming.

The frogmouth was most indignant. Couldn't a respectable bird leave its home for a moment to get food for its young without this prowling animal trying to steal that young one? Frogmouth forgot that he himself was as bad as Dasyure seeing that earlier that very night he had raided the nest of a willy wagtail and had got away with a nestling.

He whirled round on silent wings and came swooping down on the tiger cat which made a vicious swipe at him with a front paw. The frogmouth attempted to rip Dasyure with its sharp, hooked bill, but did not succeed; neither did Dasyure succeed in clawing the bird.

The frogmouth flew in a circle and then came to rest on the other side of the nest. It made harsh croaking sounds and the youngster immediately clambered out of the nest and crept along to its parent. The old bird sidled further down the branch with the nestling following it.

Dasyure watched the proceedings suspiciously and wondered what was going on. The nest was between him and the birds, but was no obstacle. He could easily hurdle that. But he was intrigued with the actions of the frogmouths, young and old, especially when the parent bird fluttered over the young one and perched on the branch between it and Dasyure. That wouldn't save either of them. Dasyure told himself scornfully.

Gradually the frogmouth nudged the young one out on to the furthest tip of the branch until the nestling was perched on a twig. Then the old bird suddenly took to the air, whirled, and came rushing at the tiger cat before that animal was properly prepared. This time it got home with a sharp rip on his back and then flew back to where the nestling was.

Dasyure was angry. Creeping along the branch, he scrambled over the nest and crouched only a few feet away from the frogmouth, whose body was hiding the youngster.

The little one was safe from the tiger cat provided it stayed where it was. Its father had got it out on to a twig that would not support Dasyure's weight. Dasyure made a lunge at the frogmouth, which skipped into the air. Then he rushed along the branch intent on getting the youngster, but when the limb began to sag under his weight, he hastily crawfished backwards.

It was at this moment that the mother frogmouth, carrying a mouse in her beak, arrived on the scene, and when she saw Dasyure squatting amid the wreckage of the nest into which he had backed to safety, she dropped the mouse and flew at him. Dasyure felt a sharp pain in the top of his head where the mother bird's beak inflicted a slight wound and then he felt talons digging into his back as the male bird screamed into the fray.

Both birds, in frantic protection of their lone baby, assailed him singly and in concert. They whirled and nose-dived, scratched and pecked, while Dasyure did his best to fend them off with his front paws. He needed his hind ones to cling to the limb.

Snarling with impotent rage, the tiger cat retreated slowly along the branch until he reached the trunk of the tree. This afforded some protection for his back. The two frogmouths alighted on the branch near the nest and eyed him balefully. Then, in an attempt to terrorise him, they protruded their feathers, flapped their wings and opened their great beaks as wide as they could, exhibiting the ugly yellow interior of their mouths. They certainly looked most alarming, but the display impressed Dasyure as much as a belligerent ant would impress an echidna.

The tiger cat measured the distance with a calculating eye and wondered if, by a sudden spring, he could pin one of them down. He knew that once he got a bird under his claws it would have little chance to escape.

He thought he could make it, and tensed himself for the spring. The nearest bird, however, must have read his thoughts, for it took off and, flying in a silent semi-circle, came down at him like a whirlwind. Dasyure saw it coming and, raising himself so that his back was pressed against the tree trunk, awaited events. The frogmouth dived straight at him, intending to try to strike him in the eyes, but Dasyure was grimly alert.

The frogmouth—it was the male bird—saw its danger too late. Unable to pull out of its dive in time, it crashed straight into the tiger cat's chest. Like lightning, Dasyure seized it with both front paws, dashed it to the limb and held it down. A quick bite finished it off.

The mother bird, still sitting on the limb near the broken nest, had witnessed the end of her mate and as Dasyure snarled and growled over the body, she took to her wings and, after circling the tree uncertainly for a few moments, alighted again, this time at the far end of the branch near the nestling.

Though he had a meal under his claws, Dasyure, for once, was not primarily interested in food. Keeping an eye on the mother bird, he slowly released his hold on her dead mate, allowing the tattered feathered ball to drop to earth unheeded. Then, in purposeful manner, he began slowly to crawl along the branch towards the mother and her youngster. He was not interested in either of them as food. All he wanted was revenge. His hide was still smarting from the wounds that had been inflicted upon him, and although the wounds were very minor ones, his passionate and proud spirit, if not his body, had been deeply wounded. He intended to inflict as much punishment as he could upon the remaining parent and, if possible, its ugly-looking young one.

The mother frogmouth watched his slow progress uneasily. She knew that she could easily elude him by just flying away, but she had the nestling to consider. She looked at it anxiously as it snuggled against her, but did not attempt to leave it.

Dasyure stopped short when he felt the branch beginning to sag under his weight. He had gone as far as he could with safety. If he proceeded further, there was every chance that the thin branch would break under his weight and send him hurtling to earth.

Glancing downwards, he noticed that the next branch was only a few feet below. He examined it carefully, half inclined to make his way down to it and see if he could do anything in the way of an upward spring from it to the frogmouths. He dismissed that idea, however, when he saw that the extremity of the branch below was just as fragile as that of the one on which he was now crouched.

As he pondered the problem, the mother frogmouth took the initiative. Springing into the air with a croaking noise, she flew in an arc which brought her back to where the tiger cat waited. Dasyure whirled round to meet her, his flashing claw weaving a protective screen in front of his eyes.

The bird shot upwards and came down hard, landing with outstretched claws on to his unprotected back. Digging her talons into his hide, she gave him a sharp peck and before he could retaliate in any way, she was aloft again.

Mad with rage, the tiger cat sat straight up on the branch and with ears laid back and teeth bared, snarled his anger. The frogmouth did not attack again, but came to rest on a limb just above his head. Dasyure shot a glare of malignant hatred at it, and if looks could kill, the frogmouth would have shrivelled up on the spot.

For a brief moment they glared at each other and then Dasyure sprang at the tree trunk and swiftly climbed to the higher branch. As soon as he reached it, the bird silently volplaned down to the other limb, this time perching near the wrecked nest.

Now the positions were reversed, the tiger cat glaring downwards at the frogmouth, and the bird almost dislocating its neck to watch its enemy's next move.

Dasyure leaned over the branch and spat curses. He realised that unless he got a lucky break, the bird would continue to have the advantage of him. Though he was at home among the treetops, he did not possess wings and the frogmouth did.

So he decided to play a waiting game. He stretched himself along the limb in such a manner that his body was hidden from the bird below. He hoped that it would be a case of "out of sight, out of mind." But the frogmouth, though it could not see him, knew he was still there, and it did not relax its vigilance.

Time passed. Dasyure did not move. It was as if he were part of the limb. The silence, as the minutes fled, began to worry the frogmouth, and its composure was more disturbed when it saw its young one sidling along the branch towards it. The youngster had become tired of its lonely existence on the far-out twig and wanted the companionship of its mother.

Dasyure, peering over, appreciated what was going on. The mother bird, watching her young one, could not also keep an eye on the overhead menace.

Standing up, Dasyure calculated his distance and sprang downwards. His front paws hit the frogmouth and sent her spinning. She wobbled uncertainly in the air for a moment, righted herself, and flew unsteadily into another tree, more frightened than hurt. But the tiger cat, unable to pull himself up, was in imminent peril of crashing to the ground. Frantically he tried to get a grip on the branch with his hind legs and tail, but the momentum was such that he shot over the limb and landed athwart the one below.

With the breath knocked out of him, he struggled to retain a precarious hold. His head was one side of the limb and his tail the other. There he hung suspended for a while like a see-saw until he succeeded in righting himself. Then he lay gasping on the limb until he felt calm enough to make a move.

Forgetful of the nestling above, he crawled along to the tree trunk and slowly scrambled down it to earth. Near the foot of the tree he found the body of the male bird which he had cast aside when he had decided to seek revenge on the mother.

Picking this up in his mouth, he made his way through the darkness towards his hollow log and, reaching it in due course, bedded down for the rest of the night after having a light supper of frogmouth. It had been an exciting and strenuous period and Dasyure was glad to turn in.

Before he finally went to sleep, however, he crawled to the entrance of the log, put his head out and stared around.

Dawn was just breaking and already the bushland was awakening with life. With a prodigious yawn, he stretched himself and then, crawling back to the centre of the log, he curled himself up, yawned again and drifted into dreamland.

CHAPTER SIX.
THE BIRD CAGE.

IT WAS AN EVENING of restful silence and the tea-tree scrub in its stillness was like a haven of peace. Now and then something moved in the thickets or a bird gave a sleepy twitter before it settled down to rest. Apart from that, all was quiet. No breeze stirred the treetops and in the west a black line of cloud lay like a barrier below the sinking sun.

Dasyure twitched his whiskers and wrinkled his nose as he crept from his hollow log. He had no set plans for the night. Something was sure to turn up. It generally did. There were very few occasions on which he returned home hungry.

As he proceeded furtively through the undergrowth and thickets he was alert for any sounds that might lead him to a feed. A rustle in the grass might betray the presence of a rabbit; the sleepy twitter of a bird in a bush could mean an easily-obtained mouthful. Nor did he neglect the ground over which he crept so silently. Creatures left tracks and he was an efficient trailer.

A mile or so from the hollow log, he took to the trees, climbing swiftly and easily up the trunk of an old ironbark, pausing for a moment when he reached the first branch. Here he gazed about him, but there was nothing edible, so he climbed higher.

In due time he reached the topmost branch. It was a profitless tree—no nests, not even a sleeping bird. He noticed a possums' nest wedged in a fork along one branch, but he was not interested in possums. They were all right in their way, but not tonight, thanks. He did not even trouble to look into the nest to see if it had any occupants.

Probably it didn't. Being night, the possums would be out and about their own business.

Dasyure did not return to the ground by the way he had come. A light spring took him across to the limb of an adjacent tree, and down the trunk of this he made his way, prospecting every branch as he did so. He found nothing and eventually reached the ground.

He was running across an open space when he paused to examine a hole. It was cone-shaped, indicating that a bandicoot had been at work. Dasyure cast around a little, but could see no tracks. The scent, too, was faint, all pointing to the conclusion that the bandicoot that had dug the hole had not done so recently.

Time was passing and the tiger cat was getting hungrier. But where was his meal coming from?

Suddenly, into his brain flashed the memory of a visit he had once paid to a farmhouse not two miles away from where he now squatted, morose and hungry.

It was a long time since Dasyure had visited the Holland farm, but he remembered the surroundings. He called to mind vividly that the poultry yard was at the rear of the main homestead, and he called to mind, no less vividly, that his departure on his previous visit had been somewhat hurried.

Sliding quietly through the fence, he crept round the house heading for the poultry run. The man-scent was everywhere, but that did not worry him. Whether the dog was still in residence or not was another matter of no moment.

When he got to the corner of the house, he peered cautiously round it. His view of the fowlhouse, however, was obscured by a large object which looked like a big box. He could not recall this having been there before.

He was creeping past it when his keen senses told him that there was a meal, possibly two, much closer than the fowlyard. The box was a large, uncovered bird cage, and his keen eyes picked out several small yellow birds, sitting side by side, some with their heads tucked under their wings, but all fast asleep.

Dasyure licked his lips as he glared at them. Now, here was something! He thrust forward a questing paw which met something hard. It was his second encounter with wire netting, though this was smaller mesh than the first. He hooked a claw into it and gave a light, experimental tug. There was very little give in the wire and he withdrew his claw, puzzled.

For a second or two he sat and stared at the sleeping birds and then he gave a sudden spring upwards, straight at them. He did not expect his outstretched paws to encounter anything except the soft feathers of his intended victims, so he was amazed and angry when those same paws hit taut wire and doubled up, allowing his nose to come into hard contact with the netting. This acted as a spring and sent him back on the ground on his haunches.

With a snarl he hurled himself again at the cage, but this time he hooked his claws in the netting and hung on. It was definitely maddening. Within inches of him was a row of birds and he could not get at them.

For a few moments he hung there motionless and just glared. As yet none of the birds had awakened. Then slowly Dasyure climbed up the wire until he reached the top of the cage which had an inverted V-shaped roof like a house. On top of this he sat for a moment and then, leaning over, took an upside-down look at the sleeping birds.

Hanging on to the roof with his hind claws, he began to pull and scratch at the wire. He did not succeed in making a hole but he did succeed in waking up some of the canaries which immediately became aware of the presence of an enemy and indicated the fact. Chirping shrilly, they began to flutter around the cage and soon every bird was awake and chirping. When one or two bumped the wire against his very claws, it was more than he could stand.

With a light leap he landed on the ground, wheeled and sprang straight at the wire again. And there he clung, impotent and filled with rage while the terrified birds set up a shrill clamour—the signal for a general disturbance. Over in the fowlyard roosters began to crow and finally Laddie, with a belated realisation of his responsibility as a watchdog, began to bark. He did not know what he was barking about, but if the canaries in the cage and the roosters in the fowlyard could kick up a row, he wanted to be in it.

Of course there could be only one sequel to this uproar. There came the sound of an opening door and out of the house and into the yard stamped the irate farmer.

"Oh, for the love of heaven, Laddie, shut up that barking and lie down, will you!" Holland roared at the dog, which immediately redoubled his efforts.

"What's going on around here?" Holland exclaimed, passionately appealing to the world at large to let him know. He walked to the corner of the house and it was then that he heard the chirping and fluttering in the bird cage. When he looked and saw a dark blob on the wire, he gave a snort of anger.

"That darned cat after the canaries again!" he muttered.

"I'll kill that useless animal one of these days. Where's a rock!"

He searched around him in the darkness for a stone or a stick to throw at the cage, but, finding none, clapped his hands and swore.

"On your way, cat, and leave those canaries alone!" he ordered, and was mildly irritated when the dark blob did not move. It was not the first time that the family cat had made a pest of itself trying to get at the canaries in the cage. There was little chance of it ever succeeding, because the wire was too strong, but that did not alter the fact that the animal was a confounded nuisance.

Dasyure, clinging to the wire with both hind claws and one front paw, was pounding away with the other trying to make a hole in the barrier. He knew, of course, that the man was there, but food was there also, and no self-respecting Dasyure since time began had allowed food to take second place to anything, even bodily safety.

Holland advanced, still clapping his hands and making shooing noises, but the tiger cat was going to see this thing through to the bitter end.

The night was dark and the farmer, even when he reached the cage and could touch the intruder with his hand, had no suspicion that it was other than his own old tom cat. He thought that Tom's claws had got caught in the wire and he could not free himself.

It was when he reached out a hand and grabbed Dasyure by the scruff of the neck that he got a rude awakening. As he gave a heave, Dasyure, still hanging tightly to the wire, twisted his head to see what had hold of him. When he saw Holland, he snarled, released his hold with his front paws, twisted his body round and inflicted two vicious scratches on the farmer's wrist.

Holland let out a sharp howl and before he had recovered

from his surprise, Dasyure, swearing to himself, was departing swiftly for the bush. When he reached the nearest tree he scaled it and, reaching a branch, squatted on it to think things out.

He hated the idea of leaving that bird cage, yet there was no profit to be gained there that he could see. It was impossible to get at the canaries. Or was it? Surely there must be some way!

After five minutes of intense brooding, Dasyure made his way down out of the tree and slid softly back to the farmhouse.

In the kitchen, Holland was thoughtfully bathing his scratched wrist in warm water. There were two long rips in his hand where Dasyure's sharp claws had scored deeply.

"It's not like old Tom to turn on you, Jack," said his wife. "What did you do to him; belt him with a stick, or something?"

"No, I did not," replied her husband. "I tried to shoo him away and when he still clung to the wire, I grabbed him by the scruff of the neck to pull him off. It was then that he turned on me. He scratched me and bolted for his life."

"I can't understand it," repeated Mrs. Holland, shaking her head. "Old Tom is not vicious. Are you sure it was old Tom? It might have been some other cat."

"Yes, and there I think you have it," said Jack Holland as he dried his hand and began gingerly to dab iodine on to the wounds. "I didn't get a really good look at the thing as it was so dark, but I wouldn't be the least bit surprised if it wasn't a tiger cat or a native cat out of the bush. Don't forget that one of them got a fowl of ours that time."

"But didn't you say that was a fox? You fired the gun at it and missed it."

"Don't rub it in," begged Holland. "Yes, at first I did

think it was a fox, but later when I examined the fowl and saw the way it had been killed, I changed my mind."

"But surely a native cat would not attack a man?" exclaimed his wife.

"Tiger cats and native cats will attack anything that comes between them and their food. Of course, I don't say that they will tackle a man just for the fun of it. That clever brother of yours says that they are afraid of nothing," said the farmer.

"Andrew would know," nodded Mrs. Holland.

"Oh, sure, he knows everything!" said Holland with a touch of sarcasm. "Anyway, he is not the only one. Old Bert Evans, the swaggie, always used to say that native cats were ruled by their tummies—that if there was a feed in sight, nothing would keep them from it. He told me that early one morning while he was camped along a creek he went out with his rifle to pot a rabbit for his breakfast and saw a tiger cat eating one. He had a shot at it and missed."

"They must be hard animals to hit with a gun," said Mrs. Holland with a laugh.

"I'll let that pass," responded her husband. "Anyway, I've never claimed to be a champion marksman. However, when old Bert missed the tiger cat it ran off into the scrub. Bert just stood there to see if it would come back and give him another shot and he got the surprise of his life when it sneaked out into the open and returned to the rabbit to resume its feed."

"What did he do then?"

"Put a bullet into it and then went looking for a rabbit of his own," replied Holland indifferently.

"But don't these native cats only go hunting at night?"

"Old Bert reckons he saw this one in daylight. He claims that they are very shy and will fight with a feather if provoked.

He admires them for their bravery."

"Well, all I can say is, he had a queer way of showing his admiration for the one he shot," said Mrs. Holland drily.

"He bowled that one over in revenge because, not so long before that, a tiger cat had killed his fox terrier."

"That takes some believing!" she exclaimed.

"Well, that is what Bert says," smiled Holland. "The old foxie was on its last legs, anyway. However, you know what these sundowners are. They like to draw the long bow a little."

"Tell lies, you mean!"

"I wouldn't say that. They merely stretch things a bit."

Holland was placing some sticking plaster over his wounded wrist when young Ted, dressed in pyjamas, entered the room, rubbing sleep from his eyes.

"What's all the excitement about, Dad?" he asked. "I got woke up by noises. Is there anything wrong?"

"Yes, some cat was after your canaries," said his father sternly. "How many times, Ted, must I tell you to cover up those birds at night? You've got a memory like a sieve."

"No old cat can break into that cage," said the lad confidently. "Why, Tom's claws are all worn out, he's so old."

"Your father thinks it was a tiger cat out of the bush, not our old Tom," put in Mrs. Holland.

"Gee, Dad, they're savage things!" exclaimed the lad. "I'd better go out and cover up the cage at once."

"You get back to bed. I'll cover the cage. Then I'll know it has been done," said his father.

"But, gosh, fancy a tiger cat coming right out of the bush after my canaries. It must have been hungry!"

"Possibly it was. Possibly you may be helping to keep it hungry, the way you go around stealing birds' eggs. You take all the eggs in the bush and the tiger cat has nothing to eat, so he comes after your canaries. Serves you right. It's only justice. It's about time you gave up saving birds' eggs. I think I'll throw them all into the fire."

"No fear, Dad!" protested Ted. "I've got the best collection of eggs in this district. I don't destroy the nests and I only take one egg when I find a nest. And, gee whizz. I hope I can find a whip-bird's nest tomorrow. I'm sure there is one in that gully in the hills."

"Never mind about that now, boy," said his father impatiently. "You get back to bed. I'm going out to cover up that cage. The canaries will probably find it hard to settle down again after the scare they have had, and the cover might help them to get a night's sleep, even if some human beings don't want to go to bed."

"See you in the morning, Dad," replied young Ted, who was a boy who could take a hint.

Holland left the house and went to a shed where he got a big corn bag. He took this to the cage and draped it over the front. The canaries were huddled together on their perch but had quietened down.

Before he went inside again, Holland had a good look round in the darkness, but could see nothing that called for investigation. He did not trouble to look at the ground. Had he done so, he might have seen Dasyure. That indignant animal was crouched at the side of the cage within a few feet of Holland's boots. He had returned to the scene not more than a minute before the farmer and now, with ears flattened and spotted body pressed close to the ground, was crouched in the angle formed by the side of the cage and the wall of the house.

He stayed there until Holland vanished round the side of the homestead and entered the back door, and then he edged his way to the front of the canary cage.

What he encountered baffled him. A few minutes earlier the interior of the cage, including the succulent canaries on the perch, had been visible, and if the man had not arrived on the scene when he did, Dasyure would have been hanging to the wire again.

The tiger cat was nonplussed. What had become of the wire and the birds? What was this blank wall that now confronted him? He clawed the hanging bag and found it soft to his touch, and when he withdrew the paw, the bag came with it for a few inches—just enough for him to see the wire underneath.

With a deft wriggle he got his head between the bag and the wire, then his front paws, and finally the whole of his body. The canaries, aware of the menace, began to protest as they had done before, causing Dasyure to lick his lips m anticipation.

His movements, however, were restricted. He was clinging to the cage wire under the bag, which rested heavily on his back. He tried to tear at the wire, but that got him nowhere. Eventually, in helpless rage, he sidled backwards from under the bag, resolving to look elsewhere for a meal.

The poultry yard! Well, he would see what that had to offer. The dog was tied up under the tree not far from the yard, but, at the moment, was dozing in its kennel. Nor did it awaken as Dasyure slid softly past.

The tiger cat was within a few yards of the hen-house when he saw a dark, slinking figure prowling through a small clump of hydrangeas that grew at the side of the building. He flattened himself to earth, his teeth bared in a snarl and his whiskers bristling. The dark figure left the hydrangeas and came strolling softly and confidently across the yard as if it owned the place. Obviously it was unaware of the tiger cat's presence, or just did not care.

Old Tom, the Holland's family cat, had been for a night's stroll in the fashion of domestic cats, and had been having an innocent yarn with a cat he knew at a neighbouring farm at the time he was being wrongfully suspected of having tried to murder the Holland canaries.

He had hardly a care in the world as he ambled across the yard and he was within three feet of Dasyure before he realised that he was not alone.

Tom was a battle-scarred old warrior who had been in plenty of fights in his time. He was also, in his own opinion but in nobody else's, a celebrated singer and, where the opposite sex was concerned, a great, romantic lover. The number of sticks, stones, boots and brushes he had stopped while singing love songs on fences and rooftops, was countless. At the moment, however, he was just a peaceful old chap going about his lawful occasions and looking for neither romance nor trouble.

He halted and looked at Dasyure with amiable curiosity. Queer sort of cat, he told himself. A stranger, too. Did not belong to any of the human families around this district. Looked as if it wanted a fight, by jove.

Tom was not afraid of Dasyure, but he did not feel in a fighting mood. Why get into a brawl if you didn't have to? He decided to be placatory so, sitting on his haunches, he uttered a friendly mew. The answering snarl he got from Dasyure caused him pained surprise. The tiger cat was in no mood for friendship, especially with this creature.

He was hungry, and this animal, whatever it was, being between him and the fowl yard, had to be removed.

Dasyure rose from the ground and glared at Tom who, taken aback, also stood up. The tiger cat gave a menacing snarl and then fell into a crouch, tensing himself for a spring. Tom decided to give the stranger one last chance to be friends before he took action. If the stranger persisted in behaving like this, then it would have to be taught a sharp lesson in good manners. His friendly mew this time had a slight edge on it and when it was answered by an ugly sort of growl, Tom became peeved.

With his tail erect like the mast of a sailing ship, his back arched and his hair sticking out like a broom, he answered snarl with snarl. Dash it, wasn't he the king of the domestic cats around here? Couldn't he belt the whole lot of them in fair fight? Obviously this stranger did not know this and had taken his overtures of friendship as a sign of weakness or cowardice. Quite definitely it had to be taught its lowly place in the scheme of things.

So the indignant Tom spat at Dasyure and waved a front paw in the air—and then found himself flat on his back with the raging tiger cat on top of him, its own claws raking lumps of fur from his stomach.

Hurt and astonished, old Tom clawed back and, with a frantic heave, threw Dasyure aside. Quick as a flash the tiger cat was on him again. Over and over they rolled—swearing, spitting, clawing, snarling and growling, with skin and hair flying in all directions.

Then, with a prodigious heave, old Tom succeeded in throwing Dasyure aside again and before the tiger cat could renew the hostilities, he was streaking past the fowl yard as fast as he could travel. Reaching the paling fence on the far side, he went up it and over the other side like a swallow.

Dasyure would have followed, though he was not nearly as swift as the domestic cat, but his attention was distracted by Laddie who, awakened by the noise of the scuffle, had emerged from his kennel and was now barking fit to kill himself. In addition to that, a door banged up at the house and a stentorian voice ordered Laddie to lie down and shut up if he didn't want his ribs kicked in.

But though Laddie had no desire to have his ribs kicked in, he neither lay down nor shut up, so Holland stormed out of the house, loudly demanding to know if everyone had gone mad that night and if he were going to get any sleep at all.

Feeling, for once, thoroughly discouraged, Dasyure gave up his idea of raiding the fowlyard and slid softly and silently towards his native bush.

CHAPTER SEVEN.

A TRAP FOR DASYURE.

Young Ted Holland was really a great lover of birds and though he did have a mania for collecting their eggs, he never destroyed a nest. The only cage birds he had were the canaries. He would never think of imprisoning the wild bush birds.

As he had told his father on the previous night, his collection was the best in the district. He had specimens of practically every bush bird, but did not possess those of the whip-bird, the white cockatoo or the black cockatoo.

Many shy birds lived in the gorge towards which he was making his way. It was several miles from his home and his many jobs around the farm—when he did them—gave him little opportunity to go exploring in distant places.

His collection of eggs had not been compiled by him alone. Old Bert Evans, the swagman, on his periodical visits to the farm, often brought the lad specimens, and Uncle Andy had given him many. But neither of them had included a whip-bird's.

Though he lived in the fern gully where there was plenty of cover, the coachwhip bird often came down to the flats in the early morning and young Ted hoped that a diligent search would reveal a nest in the gully.

Old Bert, with whom he often discussed birds, refused to mention the name, "coachwhip bird."

"His whistle is nothing like the crack of a coachwhip," he used to say. "In the old days I often heard Cobb and and Co.'s drivers in action. The bird sounds more like the swish and crack of a stockwhip. I've often been tricked into thinking there was a drover around, when it was only old Cracker."

Ted had never been able to find a whip-bird's nest, but a free day which luckily came his way, gave him the opportunity to make a proper search of the gorge, through which the creek ran.

The boy took up his position on a bank which was steep and overlooked the still, brown water, in which the overhanging trees were reflected. It was a peaceful spot.

He had not been seated long before he heard a quiet call, just "twi-twit" repeated often. He sensed that it was a bird's alarm-call and guessed that he must be close to a nest.

He got up and commenced to search the surrounding bushes carefully and there, in some thickets, he saw an open, saucer-shaped nest containing two bluish-white eggs with black markings. He stood enthralled and triumphant that at last he had found a whip-bird's nest.

And, crouched behind a bush not three yards away, Dasyure snarled hopelessly to himself. He, too, had found that nest and he wanted the contents.

The night had been worse than awful. He had not eaten a single thing. It was broad daylight and he should have been home long since sleeping in his hollow log. But how could any animal sleep contentedly when it was hungry? Two whip-bird's eggs would be precious little, but they would be better than nothing at all. Now it looked as if he were going to miss out even on those, thanks to the presence of an interfering small human being.

After leaving the farm, Dasyure had prospected the bush far and wide. There was absolutely nothing doing at all in the food line. It was as if every living creature was conspiring against him.

In his wide circuit, he had entered the gorge and though he had been as cautious as usual, his presence had been detected by the female whip-bird. Her efforts to lure him away from the spot by pretending to be wounded had been of no avail. Dasyure was up to all those tricks. Had the bird acted normally, he might have passed on without trying to disturb her, but her very protective instincts had effectually given the show away.

That the boy, too, was a most unwelcome visitor, was soon demonstrated. The mother bird, dashing past, cried out as if in pain. By pretending that she were injured, she hoped to lure Ted away from the nest in pursuit of herself. Ted, wise in the ways of birds, took no notice. He decided to leave the eggs in the nest for a while and to watch the bird. He was in no hurry. Allowing the bushes to swing back into place, thus hiding the nest, he returned to his seat on the bank of the creek.

Dasyure noted all this, but stayed where he was.

The mother bird, thinking the boy had departed, and quite forgetting the tiger cat, returned to the nest. Her mate, who was across on the other side of the creek, flew over to see what all the excitement was about. He saw young Ted and, flying on to a branch, studied him closely. Then, deciding that the lad was a menace about the place, the bird flew back across the stream where, perched on a twig, he gave his famous call, the long whistle ending with the sharp whip-crack. His mate answered him with her "twi-tweet" and every time he cracked his whip she gave the same reply.

But the male bird was very uneasy. He flew back again to where Ted was and dashed around among the trees. He made a pleasing picture. His plumage was dark bronze-green, while the crest on his head was jet black. He had white patches on his cheeks and breast and at times when he perched on a limb, he spread his tail until he looked something like a small lyrebird—except for the tell-tale black crest.

While all this was going on, Dasyure was becoming famished. There, within a few feet of him, was a nest containing two eggs and a bird sitting on them. From where he was crouched behind his bush he could just see portion of young Ted. To get at the bushes in which the nest was, he had to creep over some open ground. The male bird was still dashing around and engaging the attention of the boy.

Dasyure decided to risk it.

Ted was having an amusing time watching the frantic male bird, which had not sighted the tiger cat, but was intent on getting rid of the boy. Then, when the bird flew away across the creek again, Ted decided to collect an egg and move off. He went to the clump of bushes, expecting any moment to see the mother bird fly out in fright, and carefully pulled them apart. The nest was still there, but there were no eggs. Neither was there any sign of the mother bird.

The lad stared in wide-eyed astonishment at the empty nest and began searching round in the bushes, thinking that in some way the eggs had fallen out or had been thrown from the nest. He found nothing.

It was a very puzzled lad who eventually made his slow way homewards.

But he was not the only one on the home trail. Creeping swiftly but cautiously towards his hollow log went Dasyure, not very contented but ready to call it a day. A fat bird and two eggs made a rather unsatisfactory snack. He was still hungry.

Dasyure did not relish being abroad in the bright sunshine and as he slipped along, he pondered on the possibility of finding a nearer hollow log or even a hole in some rocks where he could sleep until nightfall. It was not compulsory for him to return to his usual dwelling place, even if there was no place like home.

Then the vagrant thought passed through his mind that he would like a taste of fish again. He had never forgotten the pleasant tang of the small perch the crane had dropped when attacked by the kookaburra. It wouldn't take him long to have a look at the place, anyway.

Turning aside, he made for the bank of the creek and eventually reached the spot where he had found the fish. There was nothing there, and the only sign of life was a cormorant, or black shag, which was sitting on the limb of a tree which projected over the water. As Dasyure watched, the cormorant dived into the creek and disappeared, presently to rise to the surface again with a fish in his beak. Tossing back his head he made short work of the morsel with one convulsive swallow, and then dived again.

Thereafter it seemed to Dasyure that all the bird did was to dive and swallow, dive and swallow. The sight did not please him. That bird was stuffing itself with food while he himself went hungry.

Eventually he turned away disconsolately, determined this time to go straight to his old hollow log and bed down for what was left of the day.

Young Ted Holland and Dasyure reached the patch of tea-tree scrub simultaneously, but the boy saw the tiger cat while the tiger cat did not see him.

Ted had been proceeding cautiously because he had caught a brief glimpse of what he had taken to be a lyrebird. These gay bush mimics always interested him and though he had often seen them at play, he never tired of watching them.

It was the habit of the lyrebird to build a mound and use it as a dancing platform. On this he would do a species of dance, at the same time imitating the calls of nearly every other bush bird. Thus it was that Ted was proceeding with great caution hoping to catch another glimpse of the elusive form he had seen, when he caught, instead, a glimpse of Dasyure.

The tiger cat, returning from the fishless detour to the creek, reached the patch of tea-tree, in the centre of which was his log home, quite ignorant of the fact that he was being closely observed by a human boy, now hiding behind a huge ironbark tree.

Ted did not move for fully five minutes after he saw Dasyure vanish into the tea-tree scrub. Then he stole from behind the ironbark and crept forward. He did not, of course, know whether he would find the tiger cat among the tea-trees or whether it had gone straight through them and beyond. But when he saw the hollow log he guessed that Dasyure was inside it. Uncle Andy had told him all about tiger cats and their habits, following the discovery of the snake-bitten body of Dasyure's mother.

The lad pondered on what he should do. The impulse to get a stick and poke it up the log was almost irresistible, but he overcame it. Though birds and their eggs were his first love, he liked all the bush animals too, and he was not a cruel boy. He had a very good idea what his father would do in the circumstances—chase the tiger cat into the open and kill it. Any argument that the wild bush creature had as much right to live as any other animal or bird, would not have appealed to the farmer. Tiger cats killed poultry and, therefore, they were neither use or ornament, in Mr.

Holland's opinion.

By jingo, thought Ted, hadn't Uncle Andy said that some people had made pets out of native cats? Gee, what if he could catch Dasyure and tame him! He could keep him in a cage until he was quiet enough to let out!

The more the lad thought of the idea, the more excited he became. But how was he to catch the tiger cat? It was a fully-grown animal and was certain to be full of fight. Ah, that was it! He would go home and make a net and put it over the hollow log entrance and drive Dasyure into it. But first he had to make sure that the tiger cat could not run away in the meantime.

Carefully and cautiously he examined the log. It was about seven feet long and two feet in diameter. One end was jammed up against a big rock, but the other was quite open and obviously was the entrance. The lad noted how hard the ground was at the entrance—trampled flat by the feet of tiger cats during the countless times they had entered and left it.

Searching around him, Ted found a big flat stone which would just about cover up the mouth of the log, and with some effort he managed to trundle it into position. It would not stand on end, so he got a stout stick and propped it up with that. It would take more than a tiger cat to shift it, he told himself with satisfaction after he had tested it.

While this was going on, Dasyure, curled up in the centre of the log, was sleeping soundly, blissfully unconscious of the plans being made for his capture and conversion into a tame domestic pet. Provided nothing untoward occurred, he would continue to sleep until nightfall.

As he hurried homewards, young Ted turned over in his mind dozens of plans for Dasyure's future. This was going to be fun, all right. So excited was he that he burst into a run, and it was not until he was almost home that doubts began to assail him.

What if his father objected to him having a savage tiger cat as a pet? He already had a dog, an ancient tom cat, and a cage full of canaries. His father and mother both often had accused him of failing to take adequate care of them. His mother especially never grew tired of telling him that if she did not feed the birds and see that the dog and cat got regular meals, they would all die of starvation. It was not that Ted was forgetful or careless, but he had grown to rely upon his mother to do all these little jobs and she, good soul, being a devoted parent who loved her young son very much, really did not mind.

He entered the kitchen to find his parents having a cup of tea and his careless air and shrill whistle did not deceive either of them.

"Well, what have you been up to now, my lad?" demanded his father sternly.

"Who, me?" asked Ted with wide-eyed innocence.

"Yes, you," said his father. "And for goodness sake, stop that whistling. Anyone would think you'd been eating the canary seed. What mischief have you been getting into?"

"He has probably been robbing more birds' nests and bringing home another cargo of rubbish to clutter up the house," sighed Mrs. Holland. "Well, Ted, how many did you steal this time?"

"None at all, Mum," replied the rueful Ted. "And they are not rubbish at all. Why, it's educational to study birds' eggs. Look at Uncle Andy."

"I don't want to look at Uncle Andy," his father said crossly. "Uncle Andy has nothing to do with it. If he wants to be a big kid running round the countryside making a goat of himself looking at birds and goannas and kangaroos, you haven't got to imitate him."

"Now, Jack, you know that Andrew's work is scientific. He is not a big kid at all," said Mrs. Holland reproachfully.

"Oh, all right, all right, don't let us argue about that," said her husband impatiently. "Just let us concentrate on young Ted here. I thought you were going to collect some greenhide eggs to add to your useless collection?"

"Greenheads?" exclaimed Ted. "I'm not interested in silly old ants' eggs, Dad!"

"Who said anything about ants' eggs?" snorted his father. "Are you trying to be funny, youngster? You know what I ought to do with all those eggs you've got?"

"Yes, Dad, throw 'em in the fire," responded Ted. "I don't think they'd burn very well, though."

"I'll prove that one of these fine days if you aren't mighty careful," warned his father. "Anyway, what is all this talk about ants' eggs?"

"You said I went out after greenheads' eggs, and greenheads are ants, Dad."

"I said greenhides, not greenheads. Birds, not ants!"

Young Ted looked bewildered.

"It was whip-birds' eggs I was after, Dad," he pointed out. "I don't know where the greenhide comes in. There are no birds of that name. I must ask Uncle Andy about them."

"Ah, I knew it was something to do with whips," said his father, with a sudden roar of laughter. "They make whip-lashes out of greenhide sometimes."

"Very funny, Jack, most amusing. You should be on the stage," said Mrs. Holland. "You know very well that the bird is not called a greenhide. But you must have your little joke, mustn't you?"

"Sometimes I could kill myself with laughter at my funny sayings," said Jack Holland with a chuckle.

"One of these days somebody will kill you for it," warned his wife. "And it will serve you right."

"I think I can take care of myself," said Mr. Holland. "Anyway, it would be a dull old world if nobody had a sense of humour."

He turned to his son. "Well, what went wrong with the hunting expedition this morning?" he asked. "Didn't you find any nests?"

"Yes, Dad, I did, and that's the funny part of it..." began Ted.

His mother interrupted him with: "Take care that your father doesn't burst into laughter, Ted. He's got a great sense of humour, you know."

Jack Holland said nothing to that.

"I found a whip-bird's nest in some grass and there were two eggs in it," Ted continued. "I left them there while I watched the parent birds for a little while. Then, when I went to get one of the eggs, they had gone. So had the mother bird who was sitting on the nest. Just vanished."

"A goanna or a snake must have sneaked up while you weren't looking and beat you to it," said his father.

"They would have had to be pretty quick to do that," said the boy.

"Of course, it is just possible that you imagined you saw the eggs and the nest," said his father. "You do imagine things at times, you know."

"He would hardly imagine a bird's nest with two eggs in it," said Mrs. Holland.

"I didn't," said Ted in aggrieved tones. "They were there all right and they disappeared. I suppose what Dad says is right—that while my back was turned a tiger cat stole them."

"I didn't say anything about a tiger cat. I said a goanna or a snake," Mr. Holland pointed out.

"Gee, Dad, it's a funny thing that you should talk about tiger cats..." began Ted, grateful for the opening.

"I'm not talking about tiger cats. I never mentioned the things," his father protested.

"I think a tiger cat would make a wonderful pet," said the boy.

His father looked at him anxiously.

"Have you got a touch of the sun, or something?" he asked. "A tiger cat would make a nice pet, would it? Yes? So would a crocodile, or a tiger snake. Or why not a nice, tame, affectionate death adder. Elephants and dingoes and gorillas also would look quite charming sleeping on the mat in front of the fire."

When he liked, Mr. Holland could be rather sarcastic. Ted tried another line.

"I saw a tiger cat in the bush today," he said carelessly. "Gee, it was pretty—brown with white spots all over it, even its tail. Ordinary native cats do not have spots on their tails, you know, only tiger cats, Dad."

"Go on, is that a fact?" asked his father politely. "You interest me greatly."

"Jack, don't make fun of the boy," Mrs. Holland chided. "It's nice for him to take an interest in animals and birds."

"Very nice," said her husband. "Very nice indeed. And it wouldn't hurt him to take an interest in his canaries and feed them occasionally, instead of leaving it all to me."

"To me, you mean, don't you?" she asked gently. Young Ted heaved a deep sigh. Here it was, all over again. Really, his parents could be trying at times!

He decided to take the plunge and short-circuit the everyday argument about feeding the canaries. "When I get my tiger cat for a pet, I bet you I'll look after him real well," he said.

"And I bet you won't, because you are never likely to have a tiger cat for a pet," said his father. "If you've got any silly ideas like that in your head, you'd better get rid of them at once, my boy."

It was going to be hard travelling, Ted told himself, but he intended to stick to his guns. "Uncle Andy says that plenty of people have them for pets," he said tentatively.

"Your Uncle Andy is liable to say anything. A nice chap, Uncle Andy, but a prize nuisance."

"No, we won't argue about Uncle Andy," he went on. with a wave of the hand towards his wife who had opened her mouth to protest. "This young fellow here is enough trouble without your admirable and scientific brother, my dear."

"Your Uncle Andrew said that he knew some people who had pet native cats that they had reared from small kittens. He said nothing about tiger cats," said Mrs. Holland.

"Yes, he did, Mum," replied the boy and then decided to take the bull by the horns. "When I was in the bush today, I saw a tiger cat..." he began.

"You've already told us that," interrupted his father.

"I was watching for some lyrebirds and the tiger cat ran into a hollow log," Ted went on rapidly and impolitely ignoring his father's comment. "I blocked up the hole in the log and I've got him trapped there. I just came home to get a net or a bag or something so that I could catch him and bring him back as a pet."

Having got out that confession, Ted stood passively awaiting the skies to fall. The skies did not fall, but his father nearly fell off his chair.

"Say that all over again, young man," he spluttered. "Kindly repeat that statement once more!"

Ted looked surprised, but obeyed.

"I was in the bush today and I thought I saw a tiger cat," he began and then stopped dead. He did not like the look on his father's face.

"Stop it!" shouted Mr. Holland. "You remind me of that silly song they used to sing on the radio, 'I tawt I taw a puddy tat'! You thought you saw it? A minute ago you said you did see it."

"So I did, too, Dad. I've got it trapped in the hollow log waiting for me to get it. Er, Dad, I don't suppose you would like to come with me and help me?"

Mr. Holland looked as if he were on the point of having six fits, one after the other, in rapid succession.

"Have you gone completely out of your mind, you silly young fool?" he exclaimed when he had recovered from his astonishment sufficiently to talk. "Got a tiger cat trapped in a hollow log, have you? You've come home to get a net or a bag to catch him, have you? You're going to bring him home as a pet, hey? And you have the colossal impudence to ask me to go and help you!"

"Yes, Dad," murmured Ted.

"Look, I've never heard anything like this in all my born days! The lad is a raving maniac! Stone the everlasting goannas, lad, you are as mad as your Uncle Andy!" bellowed the irate Mr. Holland.

"Now, now, Jack, enough of that!" exclaimed his wife. "You shouldn't lose your temper like that! And Andrew is far from insane."

"Well, if your brother Andy isn't mad, your son Ted certainly is!" said Jack Holland with conviction. "Him and his tiger cats! I suppose he'd like to keep it in the fowlhouse and save himself the trouble of feeding it!"

"They eat other things besides fowls, Dad," said Ted.

"Possibly. And I can tell you this: None of them is going

to eat anything on this farm if I can prevent it, and as long as I have a gun and the strength to pull a trigger, I'll prevent it all right," said his father violently.

"Now, Jack, calm down, for heaven's sake," begged Mrs. Holland. "As for you, Ted, don't be so ridiculous. You can't be serious about this."

"Yes, I am, Mum," said Ted.

"You cannot possibly bring home a savage tiger cat for a pet. It might be different if it were a young kitten."

"No, it wouldn't," put in her husband.

"This one isn't very big," said Ted eagerly.

"Size has nothing to do with it," his father snorted.

"You cannot possibly bring a tiger cat here, Ted," Mrs. Holland repeated. "The best thing you can do is to go straight back to the bush and let it out of the log."

"I know a better thing than that for him to do," said Mr. Holland grimly. "He can take a hoe and proceed to the potato bed and work off his insanity among the weeds there. As for the animal in the log, let it stay there."

"But if it is blocked in, it will die," protested his wife.

"And who cares about that? Possibly the tiger cat himself, but he doesn't count," said Mr. Holland. "Let the thing dig its own way out."

"It can't dig through wood, Dad," Ted pointed out.

"Off you go to the potatoes, my lad," his father instructed. "And make sure that you do go there. Anyway, I'll be down later to watch your progress. On your way."

And on his way Ted went, brooding intensely.

CHAPTER EIGHT.
TERROR IN THE BUSH.

TED WAS CALLED up from the potato patch to have his lunch and after the meal was over, his father instructed him to return there. He did.

But his mind was not on hoeing weeds. He could not prevent his thoughts from wandering into the bush to the hollow log. He felt certain that Dasyure would not be able to escape by his own efforts, because the stone across the entrance was large and heavy and was jammed hard into place with the stout stick. Probably the tiger cat would not want to get out before dark and that was many hours away yet. Something might turn up before then.

The boy wondered how long the tiger cat could live in the log without food. Uncle Andy had said that tiger cats were great eaters and thought of little else. That being so, they must need plenty to keep them going.

Any plans Ted might have had of slipping away and liberating the captive were nipped in the bud by his father who kept a sharp eye on him. Mr. Holland was not a callous man. He had little doubt that the tiger cat could escape from the log all right by just digging a burrow. He knew nothing of the animal's habits or he would have realised the impossibility of this. Tiger cats were not burrowing animals and, in any case, to dig his way out of the log, Dasyure would have to burrow through wood.

Holland's chief design was to keep young Ted working and to prevent him wandering off into the bush again to bring the captive home. He did not want any tiger cats around the house.

Ted thought of, and rejected, several excuses for leaving the potato patch. When his father joined him there and commenced to work in the next row, it simply meant that Ted had to stay there, too.

After tea that night, the youngster caused some surprised comment when he personally saw to the covering of the canary cage and then took Laddie's evening meal to him. Laddie was a venerable cattle dog who spent most of the time in his kennel. He was chained up only at night.

"I don't know why we do it," Mr. Holland remarked to his wife. "What with foxes and tiger cats and other useless animals around after my fowls, it might be a good idea to let him run loose."

"What earthly use would old Laddie be?" asked Mrs. Holland. "He is well past his prime and would probably run away if he saw even a fox."

"He's not past his prime as a noise-maker," said the farmer. "I've never known a dog to kick up as much row as that animal. All he does is loaf, eat, bark and howl."

"Which makes him a good watchdog—the barking, I mean," said Mrs. Holland.

"By the way," she added, "did you notice Ted putting the canaries to bed tonight and giving Laddie his tea? He must be reforming."

"He must be sickening for something. You can be sure

that the reformation will be very temporary," said the cynical farmer.

Ted retired to bed as usual about an hour after his tea, but he could not sleep. He was worrying about Dasyure imprisoned in the log. Long before now, he told himself, the tiger cat would have tried to get out to go on his nightly hunt. He pictured Dasyure frantically attempting to escape and slowly starving to death. It was a horrifying vision to the lad.

"It will be all my fault," he muttered. "I should have had more common sense. I should have known that Dad would not let me have a tiger cat for a pet."

The more he thought about the plight of Dasyure, the more it worried him. He lay awake and stared at the ceiling, and as he did so, a daring plan entered his head. He would get up, get dressed, go to the hollow log and let Dasyure out! He had never been in the bush before at night, either accompanied or alone, but he was not afraid. There was nothing in the bush to harm him and he could take old Laddie along. Laddie would not be of much use in an emergency, but he would be company.

It seemed to the boy that hours passed before he heard his parents retire to their room. By sitting up in bed he could see through his bedroom window and observe the patch of light thrown from his parent's room. He kept an eye on this light-patch and when it vanished, he got out of bed and quietly dressed himself.

"Gee, I'm glad it is a moonlight night," he whispered to himself. "I don't think I could face the bush in the pitch dark."

He sat on the side of the bed for about ten minutes to give his parents time to go to sleep and then, his heart in his mouth and the devout hope in his breast that his parents would not hear him, he climbed stealthily out of the window and dropped to the ground.

As he crept quietly towards Laddie's kennel, he hoped that that champion barker would not live up to his reputation and awaken the whole neighbourhood. In this he was fortunate. The old dog who was lying outside his kennel, saw him coming, recognised him, and greeted him with a wagging tail and clinking chain.

"We're going for a walk in the bush," Ted told him. "I'm keeping you on the chain because I don't want you to stray away from me and maybe get lost."

Laddie wagged his tail as if in complete endorsement of the suggestion that he was silly enough to get lost in the bush. He did not know that his young master was deceiving him, and that the plain truth was that he needed the dog's close companionship.

Ted and Laddie were quickly clear of the Holland property and making for the bush, which actually encroached upon it. They were soon in the scrub and the deeper they penetrated, the lower Ted's spirits dropped. It was rather dark among the trees. There was no fun in this and he wished heartily that he had waited until dawn before setting out on such a crazy rescue trip.

To keep his spirits from drooping right to the ground, Ted began to talk to Laddie about his collection of birds' eggs. Laddie wagged his tail courteously at the sound of his master's voice, but he was not interested in what he was saying. To the old dog this was *really* an adventure. He hadn't been in the bush for a long time, and forgotten excursions when he was a young and lusty animal flooded his brain. He strained at the chain and in spite of his age, at times literally dragged the reluctant Ted along with him. He thrust his nose into bushes, snuffled the ground, gave short, sharp, challenging barks at the moon, and generally enjoyed himself.

They were crossing a small clearing when something flew right in front of Ted's face without him hearing it. The boy gave a squeak of alarm and his blood ran cold. It was only a nightjar, the most silent creature in the whole of the bush, but its sudden appearance and disappearance was startling.

He had hardly recovered from this shock when a loud cry rent the air, apparently coming from a tree right over his head. Ted's hair stood on end and he stopped dead. The cry, or shriek, was repeated, and the lad turned to flee. He was not game to look upwards for fear that his eyes should see some frightful fiend glowering at him from the branches—perhaps a bunyip. But didn't bunyips live in creeks and swamps? He sincerely hoped so. He wished that he were home safely in bed. What mad impulse had made him embark on this awful journey?

Old Laddie was not perturbed by the strange noises. He tugged at the chain as if impatient to be on the way. Ted hauled him back and impulsively grabbed and hugged him for sheer comfort. The dog didn't get the idea, but he didn't mind—in fact he responded to his young master's caresses by licking his nose.

Feeling more at ease, Ted decided to risk looking up into the tree. He raised his head slowly and allowed his eyes to wander among the branches, but could see nothing at all. Then he heard a slight rustle and caught a glimpse of a small animal squatting on a limb about ten feet up. And as the boy stared at it, the little animal uttered the sharp cry that had scared him.

"Oh, gosh, Laddie, it's only an old possum!" he exclaimed, relief flooding over him. "Guess there's nothing to be afraid of about a possum! Come on, let's get a move on. The log is only a short distance away now."

There were no more untoward incidents before they reached the tea-tree scrub and, by the leaf-filtered light of the moon, boy and dog examined the blocked-up log. The stone was still wedged into position.

"I'm just going to knock the stone down and then we'll be off," Ted told Laddie. "I'm not going to stay in this bush a second longer than I have to."

Laddie wagged his tail and gave a short, answering bark which could have meant assent, dissent, or neither.

Dasyure, cooped up in the log, heard that bark and it certainly did not add to the sweetness of his temper. He was seething with fury.

He had awakened at dusk and, after yawning and stretching, had decided to go hunting immediately. But when he reached the entrance, he couldn't get out.

What was all this about? There was no precedence for this kind of thing. He put out a paw and touched the stone. It did not move and he looked at it thoughtfully. Then he placed both front paws on it and pushed. Nothing happened.

Turning round, he crawled to the other end of the log, but that got him nowhere because it, too, was blocked by a rock—a huge one. It always had been. Returning to the familiar entrance he searched around again for a hole to get through. There were none. He crawled up and down the hollow log several times before he realised that he was trapped.

Snarling and hissing in his fury, he hurled himself at the blocking stone and achieved nothing but a hard crack on the skull. Picking himself up, he began again to explore the log's interior. Backwards and forwards he went, over and over again, until it was driven home to him beyond all dispute that he just couldn't get out.

Retiring at last to his bed in the centre, he lay down and growled, grunted and swore to himself. It was maddening. He couldn't get out and he was ravenously hungry. And as time went on the hungrier he got. He secured very little satisfaction out of gnawing some ancient rabbit bones in his lair.

And then he heard the dog bark. Instantly he became alert, tense and watchful. In his very soul he felt that danger lurked very near him.

His attention became concentrated upon a noise at the entrance to his home—or where the entrance should be. Something was there and something that boded evil for him.

Dasyure, ears back, teeth bared in a snarl, crouched and awaited events, ready to fight anything that presented itself.

On the outside, young Ted had pulled the supporting stick aside and that was the noise the tiger cat had heard. The rock still stood upright, and the lad took hold of it and lowered it to the ground. Then he pushed it aside a few feet. That ought to do it. He couldn't see any reason why he should carry it back to where he had found it.

In order to have both hands free to move the stone, Ted had to drop Laddie's chain. Not desiring to be left out of what was going on, the old dog marched forward and thrust his nose into the entrance to the log.

"Come away from there, Laddie," Ted ordered, but Laddie took no notice of the order. He was a dog that rarely did what he was told. He gave a couple of sniffs and then barked an inquiry. There was something in the log and he burned with curiosity to know what it was.

Crouched inside, Dasyure saw the dim patch of light that told him freedom was near. No longer was there a barred door to his home. He did not know how this had come about, but he did know that he was leaving immediately, irrespective of what might be waiting for him outside.

He began to creep forward, and as he did so, two golden lights appeared at the door. Dasyure knew what they were—the eyes of some animal. Probably the animal that had blocked him in. Fine! The tiger cat yearned to discuss his imprisonment with the creature responsible.

Dasyure was vastly angry and his anger did not diminish when the creature made a loud noise. He recognised that noise. It was the bark of a dog. Hadn't he heard quite enough of barking dogs when he had visited the Holland farm?

With a rush he reached the entrance of the log and barged straight into the startled Laddie, inflicting two deep scratches on the dog's nose with his sharp front claws. The astonished Laddie gave a yelp and then went head over heels as Dasyure knocked him flying.

The enraged tiger cat hurled himself on top of the dog and began biting and ripping his hide. Laddie howled with pain and shock and made only feeble attempts to retaliate. He was now lying on his back with Dasyure on top of him, snarling, grunting and worrying him.

Under the horrified gaze of young Ted Holland, the two animals, large and small, rolled over and over on the ground. Dasyure was snarling and spitting, but the noise he made was as nothing compared with Laddie's yelps and howls. The old dog was more scared than hurt, though the tiger cat had succeeded in getting home a few painful nips and scratches.

Scarcely knowing what he was doing in his excitement, Ted grabbed the stick he had used to prop up the stone in front of the hollow log, and began to strike the contestants impartially. The stick was rather short for such work, but he did his best with it. Sometimes Dasyure collected a whack and sometimes Laddie did, but it did not bring the contest to an end.

Throwing the stick aside, Ted seized the dog's chain and began to heave. By this means he managed to drag Laddie to his feet, Dasyure clinging to the dog. Ted wound the chain towards him and when the combatants were close enough, he held the chain firmly in one hand while he retrieved the stick with the other. Then, watching his chance, he whacked Dasyure every time he could get a fair and clear hit at him.

After half a dozen such hits, the tiger cat woke up to the fact that he was fighting a boy as well as a dog, and when Ted fetched him an extra powerful whack across the head, he decided to withdraw from the contest. Inflicting a final bite upon the dog, he relaxed his grip, threw a parting snarl at Ted, and then slipped away through the tea-trees to the safety of the dense scrub beyond.

Ted allowed him to depart and then examined old Laddie. The ancient dog had a few minor wounds but did not appear to be much hurt, except in his feelings.

"There now, boy, he's gone," said Ted soothingly. "Nothing more to fear from him."

Saying which, the boy patted Laddie and stroked his coat. Laddie rewarded him by licking his hand and wagging his tail feebly.

"Come on, boy, let us get home as fast as we can. I've had enough of this bush," said Ted with a slight shudder as he looked around. Though it was moonlight, the bush was beginning to take on a sinister aspect.

"Gosh, Laddie," he said as they walked along, the boy hanging on to the chain like grim death, "fancy me wanting that tiger cat for a pet. I must have been as silly as a wet hen, mustn't I?"

Laddie's short bark was one of complete agreement.

Ted was feeling very indignant towards Dasyure. He did

not like the tiger cat for its fight with Laddie, and he really did feel that the bush creature had let him down badly. He could not have explained clearly what he meant by that, but it appeared to him that the ungrateful tiger cat had betrayed him. He had been willing to find a good home for the animal and it had repaid him by attacking his dog. There was no gratitude in the world after that!

"Ah, well, Laddie," said the boy, "we've had more than enough for one night. Thank goodness we are almost home. Let us hope it will be a peaceful trip from now on."

"Here, here!" barked Laddie.

But it was not to be.

They were about a quarter of a mile from the homestead and were passing a clump of about a dozen banksias, when from out of the very centre of these trees came a terrible scream as if someone were being tortured.

As the horrible cry echoed through the quiet night, young Ted's blood chilled in his veins, while all the hair on Laddie's back stood straight up. With a yelp of sheer fright, the dog bounded away, nearly pulling Ted's arm from its socket. The boy, however, clung like glue to the chain, bringing Laddie to a sudden halt and nearly strangling him.

Ted was rooted to the spot. Terror gripped him and no power on earth seemed capable of giving him the gift of swift departure.

Then once again the silence was shattered by the horrible scream from the banksias. Laddie gave a convulsive leap and this time succeeded in wrenching the chain from his young master's grasp. Then he bolted through the trees as if every fiend in existence were hot upon his trail.

With a yell that almost rivalled those he had heard in the banksias, Ted at last managed to get his feet to work, and he shot off in swift pursuit of Laddie.

And as he departed, the "victim of the torture," who had uttered the terrifying cries—a powerful owl perched on the sloping branch of a banksia, flew off on silent wings, somewhat surprised at the actions of the boy and the dog.

There was no sign of Laddie when Ted panted up to the house. That stricken animal was crouched in his kennel thinking things over and wondering what was going to happen next. It had been an exciting and rather unnerving night for him. After all, he was a venerable dog of regular and peaceful habits, and such adventures as he had gone through were just a trifle unsettling.

Ted scrambled through the open window of his bedroom and, pulling it down and locking it, quickly tore off his clothes and slipped into bed.

It was a long time before sleep came to him. Had somebody been tortured in the bush? It was not a nice thought by any means. He could not tell his parents about it, because they would want to know what he had been doing wandering around the bush in the middle of the night.

"I guess it must have been a bird or an animal," he told himself, "but I'm blessed if I've ever heard of one that makes those noises. Anyway, there is one thing I do know—I'm not ever going near that place again, or near the jolly old tiger cat's home."

And it was with this firm resolve that the lad fell asleep.

CHAPTER NINE.
DASYURE'S NEW HOME.

AFTER LEAVING the scene of conflict, Dasyure blundered along through the bushes and thickets in an almost aimless fashion. Though quite unhurt bodily, he was still wild with anger and indignation, and did not seem to care where he was going.

This mood possessed him until he reached the bank of the creek. There he paused and looked around him. A soft wind sighed through the reeds and the stream itself looked very peaceful in the pale moonlight. Dasyure tested the air with upraised nose, but could scent nothing that might be eatable.

Slowly and carefully he crept through the reeds and bushes which grew in profusion along the bank, pursuing a course parallel with the stream. His investigations revealed neither birds nor small animals nor other edible things.

Reaching an open space, he stole down to the edge of the creek and had a drink of water. He was turning away when he heard a very slight rustle in the reeds to the right. and his keen eyes instantly detected the cause of it—a native water-rat. The little animal was making for the creek and had about a dozen feet to go to reach it.

Between the water-rat and Dasyure was a few square yards of mud and grass—not very good cover for the tiger cat.

Dasyure made a rapid calculation. Perhaps a swift rush and spring would accomplish his purpose. He gathered himself for the effort and was on the point of taking off when the water-rat saw him. It had covered half the distance to the creek and as Dasyure made his leap it hastily scampered to the edge of the water and dived straight into it, to disappear below the surface.

The disappointed tiger cat rushed to the spot and glared anxiously into the water. Keen though his eyes were, they could not penetrate the brown depths. Then he noticed a small dark blob a few yards out from the shore. It was the head of the water-rat which had come to the surface and was swimming strongly towards the opposite bank.

Dasyure was half inclined to dive in and follow it, but he was no swimmer and quickly gave up that idea.

Retiring to the reeds again, he squatted down morosely. Far out on the moonlit creek he could still see the small blob that marked the water-rat's head. It was now close to the other bank.

Dasyure was thinking of moving away when his attention was attracted by a whirring of wings and out of the sky and down to the creek surface swept four birds. They had hardly settled, however, before they went splashing away up the creek, using their wings like steamer paddles and not rising from the surface. They travelled at a great rate for perhaps a hundred yards and then, swinging round, clattered and splashed their way back again until they finally came to a halt opposite Dasyure.

These birds were musk-ducks, and they had long and narrow tail-feathers just like spikes. Though they were well able to fly, they rarely did so, preferring to splash along like speed-boats. But when they travelled from one waterhole to another, or from a creek to a swamp, they used their wings in the orthodox manner and flew like other birds.

Dasyure, watching them swimming around, wished heartily that one of them would come near enough for him to capture; but it was hardly likely that any of them would. That was not his luck.

He sat and watched them broodingly as they floated on the water. Then, all of a sudden, there was a flurry of feathers and spray and one of them disappeared beneath the surface. The other three, taking alarm at something, clattered away up the stream and were soon lost to sight.

Intensely interested, Dasyure watched them vanish, and then turned his attention again to the spot where the fourth had disappeared below the water. There it was again, in plain sight, but it was not swimming. It was lying on its side as if dead. What had happened to it?

As the tiger cat watched, the dead musk-duck began to move slowly towards the shore in his direction. What was all this about?

He got up and stole towards the edge of the water. If this dead duck floated ashore, he intended to make a meal of it.

Dasyure got another surprise when he reached the water's edge. The bird was not floating shorewards, but was being towed by a water-rat—probably the same animal he had seen previously. The rat had killed the musk-duck by biting through its spine at the head and was now, presumably, dragging it home to eat. The tiger cat, however, was determined that if that musk-duck were going to provide a meal for anybody, it was not going to be for a native water-rat. No, not while an able-bodied and hungry tiger cat was around!

In order to give the water-rat no clue to his presence and thus give the show away, Dasyure crouched behind a convenient tuft of grass and, from this vantage point, watched the proceedings with anticipatory interest.

Though the water-rat was not large, it was strong, and when it got the musk-duck to shore, immediately commenced to tow it up the gently-sloping bank.

Dasyure waited until the water-rat had gone about three feet and then, leaving the shelter of the tuft of grass, walked calmly and confidently over to it.

The water-rat took one look at him and then went for its life. Dasyure was too big a proposition for it to handle. The tiger cat sniffed at the bird and though he did not go much on its strong musky smell, picked it up in his mouth and retired to the top of the bank where, at his leisure, he ate as much of it as he fancied. When the last bone had been crunched and the final feather spat out, Dasyure licked his chops appreciatively, gave a satisfied yawn and ambled away down the creek bank. It would soon be time to look for a place to sleep. Dawn could not be very far away.

Dasyure was fully resolved never again to return to his old hollow log in the tea-tree scrub, or even to the old familiar hunting grounds. He had done with all that for good. Now that his retreat had been discovered, and by human beings, there could be no safety there in the future. Added to that, the old hunting territory had become a harder place in which to obtain regular square meals. No, he intended to find a new home and new hunting grounds.

He discovered a small cave in the side of a hill about one hundred yards from the creek bank, and there he bedded down. It was not much of a place and certainly would not do for a permanent home. It would, however, serve for one day's sleep.

At dusk he was on the move again and heading west-wards, following the creek. He travelled most of the night, pausing only to make a meal of a rabbit that he trapped in a small gully. Dawn found him seven or eight miles from the old hollow log and once again it was necessary for him to find a sleeping place.

He was still in the gully in which he had trapped the rabbit. It was walled in by banks about ten feet in height, and there was a shallow watercourse in the middle. This joined the creek half a mile away, but was more often dry than not. It was, in reality, a drain for rainwater running down from the hills in wet weather.

Dasyure decided to climb up the gully wall and seek out a hole among the many rocks he could see above him. He went along a well-defined pad leading upwards and halfway up the rise came upon a large hole at the edge of the track.

He turned aside and inspected it with a critical eye. It might make a very comfortable residence. By the marks on the ground it belonged, or had belonged, to a wombat, but that did not matter. If there was another dweller in occupation, it could easily be ejected. Dasyure had no doubts about his ability to dispose of any occupant.

Proceeding cautiously, he entered the hole, which had an arched doorway. It led straight into the hillside and was about seven feet deep. At the end was a comfortable nest of bark and dry grass. Just the very thing! Dasyure lapsed into the nest, yawned, and promptly went to sleep.

He had been in the land of dreams for five minutes when he was rudely awakened by a sharp nudge in the ribs. The rightful owner of the burrow, a wombat, had returned home.

Dasyure was in a fix. The new arrival was three times as large as he was, and it had him squashed into the nest with no hope of escape. Its body filled almost the entire circumference of the burrow.

With a hoarse, growling cough of resentment, the wombat

gave Dasyure another heavy bunt with its snout and then drew back to have a look at him.

This was precisely what the tiger cat required—a little space in which to manoeuvre. There was still not enough room for him to spring, but at least he was not squashed up against the end of the tunnel. He promptly seized the end of the wombat's nose with his strong teeth and bit it as hard as he could.

Grunting with pain, the wombat drew back still further and Dasyure, with a vicious snarl, hurled himself on to his opponent and, having raked its face with both front claws, again bit it.

And although the wombat was three times the size of the tiger cat, it turned tail and fled, Dasyure biting and scratching its rear as it went.

The unfortunate wombat reached the entrance to its former home and rushed down into the gully. Dasyure did not follow it. He stood at the mouth of the burrow and watched it go.

The wombat paused when it reached what it considered to be a safe distance, and looked up. The tiger cat waved a paw at it and gave a derisive snarl. That snarl conveyed to the wombat the intelligence that it would return at its peril—that the burrow in the hillside was now the country residence of a tiger cat.

The wombat had a great affection for that gully. It liked the surroundings and it liked its burrow. It appeared, however, as if that were gone for good. Most depressing, of course, but there were other spots just as good and a new home would be easy to dig in the gully.

Watched by Dasyure, the wombat selected another site on the opposite side of the gully and, lying on its side and using its powerful front paws, began to excavate a hole with its strong, shovel-like nails. As it dug it thrust out the soil with its hind feet.

This did not suit Dasyure at all. He did not want the wombat as a neighbour. He wanted the whole of the gully to himself. Wherever he lived he insisted on being monarch of all he surveyed.

Leaving the mouth of the burrow, he dropped down to the gully floor and scrambled across to the other side. The busy wombat did not know he was there until he felt the tiger cat's sharp teeth in his hide.

Hastily withdrawing from the hole he was digging, he turned round and made a rush at his small attacker. Dasyure side-stepped with some agility and then sprang on the wombat's back. There he clung like a limpet, digging his claws into the other's fur. In an effort to dislodge him, the wombat rolled over and over on the ground, but Dasyure had neatly dropped off at the first sign of the rolling.

No sooner had the panting wombat righted himself than the tiger cat was on his back again. Dasyure was now thoroughly enjoying himself. The wombat tried to get rid of him by rubbing him off against the gully wall, but did not succeed.

Finally, in sheer despair, he set off at a lumbering trot down the gully, the tiger cat clinging to him and biting and clawing.

Dasyure dropped off when the wombat reached the entrance to the gully and watched the lumbering form until it vanished into the bushes down near the creek. And as the tiger cat made his way back to the stolen burrow, something told him that he would never see the badger-like animal again.

In that he was perfectly correct. The wombat, thoroughly disgusted, was fully resolved that wild horses would not drag him back to the scene of his discomfiture.

Dasyure stalked like a king into his new home and surveyed the interior with an immense amount of satisfaction. He felt on the best of good terms with himself. He had a brand new residence, a comfortable bed, an entirely new territory in which to hunt—a territory, as far as he knew, uncontaminated by human beings—and he had put to flight an enemy three times as large as himself. Truly, he was a magnificent marsupial!

Having indulged in this piece of self-admiration, he went to the entrance of the burrow again and admired the scenery.

The sun was just rising above the hills, shedding its glorious light upon a glorious world. In the distance he could see the willows and tea-trees that marked the course of the creek. High in the blue above hovered a hawk, its keen eyes raking the earth below for a victim. Dasyure, regarding it benevolently and with fellow-feeling, hoped that it would make its kill. Into some acacia trees on the opposite bank flew a swarm of little finches. Finches, Dasyure reflected, built nests, laid eggs and hatched young ones. That meant meals for him.

Unquestionably, it was a good world!

Turning round, he walked jauntily and with tail erect,. down the burrow to the nest of bark and dry grass. Into this he dropped with an air of proprietorship that would have maddened the poor old wombat.

Yawning mightily and then blinking sleepily, he curled himself up, his ears flattened and his spotted tail across his nose.

Then, in his supreme contentment, Dasyure, the tiger cat, went to sleep.

THE END

ENJOY THIS BOOK?

BE SURE TO CHECK OUT THESE OTHER GREAT TITLES FROM THE SAME AUTHOR AT WWW.LIVINGBOOKPRESS.COM

ARRIGAL THE WARRIOR

The story of a killer-dog. His owner had tried to train him to the domestic life, but the call of the wild and his hunting instincts were too powerful. As a killer he roamed abroad, hunted fiercely by farmers whose stock he wantonly destroyed. It is a story that is founded in fact.

As for Warrigal — he is as nature fashioned him.

"I have not sought to glorify Warrigal, neither have I condemned him. I have just tried to present him as he really is, without fear or favour, affection or ill-will."

WOMBAT

Clumsy old Bill the wombat, the grumpiest creature in the bush, is a positive pain in the neck and a great nuisance to police trying to investigate the theft by two thieves of a Chinese treasure box. The police are also pestered by two small boys, lovable but mischievous young rascals, and by several suspiciously-acting and inscrutable Chinese. It is grumpy old Bill the wombat however, and his feathered and furred bush friends who take the centre of the stage and provide a great deal of the comedy and excitement.

Authentic as to detail, the book provides young readers with much information about the interesting marsupial wombat, a creature hitherto neglected by Australian natural history writers.

WILLY WAGTAIL

Is there any Australian who does not know that friendly little chap, the black and white fantail? Go where you will, in crowded city park, in suburban backyard, or in the heart of the lonely bush, there he is, the companion of everyone, Willy Wagtail, the bush newspaper and busybody, minding everybody else's business as well as his own.

In this light-hearted story of the great open spaces, Willy gets himself in and out of a lot of strife. He is ably assisted in his nuisance-making by a wide variety of bush birds and animals, as well as a quartet of small boys, all of whom have their own troubles without a wagtail adding to them.

Such doings are most deplorable, but they make excellent reading for young and old.

WILD CANARY

Here is a natural history story for children that is certain to cause many a friendly—and maybe not so friendly—argument among bird lovers of all ages. Can an ordinary, commonplace canary, born and bred in a cage like his ancestors for hundreds of years before him, survive the many perils of the bushland?

Mr. Thompson has a sound knowledge of our native birds and animals and he is also, personally, an enthusiastic canary breeder. He now matches one against the other in a series of adventures, grave and great, that "could have happened".

Thousands of Australian children who own and love their pet canaries, will read with absorbing interest this exciting tale of a canary freed from captivity during a disastrous flood and its successful fight for existence in competition with the hardy bush denizens.

THUNDERBOLT THE FALCON

When Joe discovers that his friend David's grandfather used to train hawks just like in the book he's reading he wants to try it for himself. After convincing Grandfather Mannering to teach them the art of falconry they set off to capture a juvenile Peregrine Falcon and learn the ancient art.

Set in Australia, but relevant everywhere Peregrine Falcons are found, Thunderbolt the Falcon is a fascinating and humorous read. C.K. Thompson weaves many facts about birds and nature seamlessly within the narrative with many events inspired by real life.

RED EMPEROR

The story of a Red Kangaroo and his adventures on the great plains of the west. A book full of thrills for the children, and one of great educational value.

Those who remember "King of the Ranges" will find this story of a Red Kangaroo just as good as its famous predecessor. It is full of wholesome adventure and includes much about our native animals that Australian children ought to know.

Like Joey, the Range King, Arunga the Red Emperor is no ordinary kangaroo. In comradeship with a grey friend, he has some startling and amusing adventures.

MONARCH OF THE WESTERN SKIES

Monarch of the Western Skies is the exciting story of a wedge-tailed eagle, from the nest until it becomes a giant bird of prey, the undisputed king of the air with a wing-span of over seven feet.

Set in the great plains and mountains of the West, this story will bring to life the story of these magnificent birds as only C.K. Thompson can.

OLD BOB'S BIRDS

Join Old Bob the sundowner and his two small friends, Roddy and Susan, as Bob shares the vast lore of the bush, gained during a lifetime of wandering.

For over 60 years readers of Australian nature stories have recognised that "Thompson and truth" are synonymous. He writes about his birds and animals as they are and not as fancy would fashion them; thus, "Old Bob", though a great bird lover, does not see his feathered friends through rose-tinted glasses. Like humans, says "Old Bob", the birds all have their little faults. Some of them, indeed, are real villains.

Written in the author's usual captivating style, these stories cannot fail to have a wide appeal. Needless to say, they are well leavened with the irresistible Thompson humour.

A library without this book of our better-known bush birds is a library incomplete.

MAGGIE THE MAGNIFICENT

"Maggie the Magnificent" is something entirely different in children's nature stories. Readers of previous books by this author have realised that he approaches the popular theme of Australian bird and animal lore from an angle never before attempted by a writer of Juvenile books—sheer entertainment deftly combined with authenticity of detail.

The birds do not talk, but they LIVE. "Maggie the Magnificent" is an exceedingly well-written story of Australia's most popular black and white bird, the magpie. Though Maggie himself is the chief character and his life and adventures are portrayed faithfully, we meet a number of humans who are drawn so naturally that they might be your next door neighbours.

Though designed primarily for the child mind, adults will appreciate the story as a rich page torn from the diary of their grandparents childhood.

TIGER CAT

This is the story of the young tiger cat's coming-of-age: of his first groping steps towards manhood after his mother's death, and how he learned to fend for himself in an unkind, uncaring world. Like many human beings, Dasyure was a shy fellow. In his habits he resembled a burglar, coming out to work only when night closed over the bush.

However, unlike the burglar, he was both brave and bold; would take on a creature whom he had no chance of beating, so pugnacious was his nature. In the story, Dasyure is both hero and villain, but as the author says: "You must have a kindly feeling towards him as a fellow-Australian. Tiger Cats, Native Cats and the rest of the Dasyuridae family do a great deal of useful work in keeping down vermin, from mice to rabbits.

BLACKIE THE BRUMBY

Wild horses and wild outlaws. Horse-thieves and "bobbies and bushies". What youngster does not love them?

Though he adheres to his fidelity of detail in depicting the lives and habits of the brumbies—the wild horses of outback Australia—the author really gets going after Blackie the Brumby is captured and tamed. He is stolen by bushrangers, takes part in their notorious doings, gives a helping hand (or hoof) to the police and, with a hilarious boy character named "Jonah", takes a leading part in the final overthrow of the gang.

KING OF THE RANGES

This story tells of Joey, a small kangaroo, whose mother is killed before she can fully impart to him all that knowledge that bush creatures need in order to fend for and protect themselves.

Joe goes through many trials—attack by men and by dingoes, capture, gunshot wounds—before he comes to rule his fellows, and by a hard-won victory over a rival animal, becomes King of the Ranges.

www.ingramcontent.com/pod-product-compliance
Lightning Source LLC
Chambersburg PA
CBHW072150020426
42334CB00018B/1942